THE LANGUAGE OF BLOOD

THE
LANGUAGE
OF BLOOD

[a memoir]

Jane Jeong Trenka

**BOREALIS
BOOKS**

Borealis Books is an imprint of the
Minnesota Historical Society Press.

The Minnesota Historical Society
Press is a member of the Association
of American University Presses.

www.borealisbooks.org

Manufactured in the United States
of America

10 9 8 7 6 5 4 3 2 1

♾ The paper used in this publication
meets the minimum requirements
of the American National Standard
for Information Sciences—Permanence
for Printed Library materials, ANSI
Z39.48-1984.

International Standard Book Number
0-87351-466-1 (cloth)

Calligraphy for chapter numbers
by Nellie Chao.

*Library of Congress Cataloging-in-
Publication Data*

Trenka, Jane Jeong, 1972–
The language of blood : a memoir /
Jane Jeong Trenka.
  p. cm.
ISBN 0-87351-466-1 (alk. paper)
1. Trenka, Jane Jeong, 1972–
2. Trenka, Jane Jeong, 1972—
   Childhood and youth.
3. Korean American women—
   Biography.
4. Korean Americans—Biography.
5. Adopted children—United States—
   Biography.
6. Intercountry adoption—United
   States—Psychological aspects.
7. Korean American children—
   Cultural assimilation.
8. Minnesota—Biography.
9. Seoul Region (Korea)—Biography.
I. Title.

E184.K6T74 2003
977.6′004957′0092—dc21

                    2003005135

Parts of this book have been published,
in slightly different versions, in *Carriage
House Review, Off the Wall*, and *Water-Stone*.

Quotations from the Child Welfare
League of America are from pamphlets
found in the Social Welfare History
Archives collection, located in the Elmer
L. Andersen Library at the University
of Minnesota. Quotations from Inter-
national Social Service and the Task
Force for Adoptive Parents are from
pamphlets found in the International
Social Service/ American Branch
records in the Social Welfare History
Archives at the University of Minnesota.

Quotation from *I Lock My Door Upon
Myself* by Joyce Carol Oates copyright
© 2002 by Ontario Review, Inc. Used
by permission.

Dialogue from *The Jerk* copyright
© 2003 by Universal Studios Publishing
Rights, a division of Universal Studios,
Licensing LLLP. All rights reserved.
Used by permission.

Quotation from *The Woman Warrior* by
Maxine Hong Kingston used by permission of the author.

"Anonymous 913" from *Classical Korean
Poetry: More than 600 Verses since the
12th Century*, translated by Jaihiun Kim,
copyright © 1995 by Asian Humanities
Press, an imprint of Jain Publishing
Company, Inc.

Designed & set in type by Cathy Spengler,
Minneapolis. Printed by Maple Press,
York, Pennsylvania. The type is Albertina,
designed by Chris Brand in 1965.

. . . Because we are linked by blood,

and blood is memory without language.

[JOYCE CAROL OATES, *I LOCK MY DOOR UPON MYSELF*]

THE LANGUAGE OF BLOOD

Dear my daughters, Mi-Ja, Kyong-Ah!

I wish Father, Mother in U.S.A. are in good health and enjoy increasing prosperity in the present business in 1992.

One year had passed and the 20 years already passed after sending you to the United States is unfamiliar. I was in pain due to your difficult conditions.

Let me try to recall my home's sad story. It was not a happy home even before our separation.

In winter cold, snowy 1964 year, I got married to your father, but your father already had two daughter, Sun-Mi and Sun-Yung between the past some woman. However, I did my best to make our happy, peaceful home since then.

Your father was a carpenter in the job site with a normal salary. He could not spend even one day without drinking. And so we had to live the monthly rent house. But, I understood your father's drinking resulted from the tired job.

After several years, your sister, Eun-Mi, was born and Mi-Ja also some years. Our family consisted of six persons at that times.

When I saw your drunken father everyday, I felt regretful. So, I tried to be helpful for your father's job. For instance, I did my best support as dealing in rice at the job spot in the southern part Jinhae of Korea.

In spite of my efforts, usually he was not satisfied with home and troubled the family members as using violence upon arriving home. Naturally, other family members were afraid of him. The neighbors laughed scornfully regarding him as a patient of morbid suspicion about wife's chastity. The habits was getting worse, as time goes by. Even though many difficulties, I made efforts to manage my home and took care of my daughters to be pretty, successful in the society.

As time goes by, your sister, Sun-Mi, entered Middle School and so I was so pleased. I hope your studying to be a proud daughter against my poor study, Middle School and High School Course. But Sun-Mi didn't follow my hope and finally deviated from the right path and runned away from home as quitting the school.

Sun-Yung, also, didn't pursue mother's hope and throwed away the study and made home noisy due to your father's indifference about home education. I was desperate in this difficult situations what to do for my home.

While living at the monthly rent house, I had to do many things to be survival by overcoming lots of troubles. I dealed in the rice cake at a barrack and sold trivial goods by carrying packs without fixed house. I had to live from hand to mouth as standing many difficults.

However, your father was always drinking and bothering family members as a slave. At last, I escaped to the house of your mother's parents because of severe violence from your father. In a few days, I was taken hold of your father. Your father apologized to me for his wrongdoing by writhing in blood come about his fingers. He swore, "I was regretful my past wrongdoing!" and "I will not do any longer!" he appealed to me make home again. "My pitiful circumstances," "My sad tears," "My sorrow," but I made a decision to live again resigning myself to my fate. Unfortunately, your father's mental sickness recurred even in a few months.

Kyong-Ah was born. I had both her under the cold winter in outdoors while other people generally bore their babies in the hospital & clinic for fear of a hindrance of mother's health. But, in my case, Can you guess my health after bearing my baby (Kyong-Ah) in the subzero temperature of 10 of cold winter night. I could be barely saved from death with neighbor's help.

But, your father was saying "Who is father!" "She is not my baby!" It was like a bolt from the blue. Your father tried to suffocate Kyong-Ah as using a comforter. It was so miserable that I couldn't explain.

As a result, I could not help entreating your father not to do like this, but he was rejected my opinion, "There is not fault to baby" by force. So, I had no solutions to persuade your father.

I was planning to send Kyong-Ah to an orphanage which is social welfare center with our neighbor's help.

In several days, I visited an orphanage located at Wooyi-dong, Seoul in order to meet Kyong-Ah due to my prostrate mind and found Kyong-Ah on the brink of death.

There were no other alternatives in this separated conditions from mother including food supply, hygienic problems not to be in the brink of death. I was almost moved to tears upon seeing the miserable conditions of my baby.

I requested a permission to take Kyong-Ah home, your father suggested some conditions, "Kyong-Ah should be sent to the United States as an adopted daughter with Mi-Ja." "I would see Kyong-Ah before going to the United States." After all, he accepted my opinion by presenting the above conditions.

Fortunately, Kyong-Ah revived after taking care of me home in 1 month.

One month later, Mi-Ja & Kyong-Ah could go to the United States on condition of a sibling adoption from an adoptive parents in U.S.A.

When you and us in the Kimpo Airport to go to the America, Kyong-Ah was in our bosom didn't know all the things and Mi-Ja was in my side, singing a song "My

Lived Home" and you left us far from here, Korea. When you had left my side and heard your song. I felt sad so much will now. During come back home, I couldn't get over my mind.

Then, your father changed in many ways and he regretted his past days and faults. He tried to be faithful with family. So in the several years, we've got some changed life and Myoung-Hee was born these days. On the other hand, I thought that I decided bear another baby but there's a reason that a Thought of Boy First in Korea. While Myoung-Hee was growing up, there's nothing to particular to us.

During several years, we asked and tried to touch with you many times but we had not hear about your safety even the orphanage, playing a mediation role. They wanted to wait for an opportunity.

Time went fast, Eun-Mi finished the three year full course the Middle School and High School but the High School wasn't a commercial or technical school, she couldn't get a job easily. She worked hard as a bus girl or as a girl of bakery shop etc.

When we worked hard for my family, your father get in the habit of drinking again. The Whirlwind rose at my home. Eun-Mi was beaten her leg with a beer bottle by your father and she had to see a doctor for 2 weeks. Besides, Myoung-Hee met with an accident by bus but your father wasn't concerned about everythings. It is no concern of him, it seemed. Your father, or more accurately the drunkard was not human and your parents.

One day, when your uncle (he is my brother) came to meet Myoung-Hee in the Hospital, your father kicked your uncle under the stairs and uncle was seriously hurt by your father's mad actions. I'm sure that your father had gone mad indeed.

There are many things about your father's bad stories

but I can't tell you in details. Because I don't want to image and it is very difficult to explain with you.

Several months went by. We moved into Seocho-Dong in Seoul and your father continued rough, assault and battery and obdurate. Your father was always bother us. One day, in the middle of the night, your father, in a drunk away, left home after a warning that he'll kill your uncle. When your father was about to thrust a bayonet through a uncle's body, your uncle fought up against your father desperately. Your father also beaten me and he was about to kill me again. We were so fear we could not let him freely.

As a result, we called a policeman for the law and your father was in a prison for six months with crime against his family and family mistreatment. During his staying in the prison, he was so angry he went on muttering that he will kill us after freedom of the law. We trembled with fear and we decided escape from your father, Eun-Mi and Myoung-Hee.

When your father got free, he looking for a chance to find us under the ground of Residence Register Card and we had to went on moving here and there to refuge from your father without any signs for about 10 years.

In the mean time, we managed to get along up to date in the vinyl house, a little hut, looks like pauper the meanest among the city of Seoul.

On reflection, I think life is short and long.

If we have a happy life, we must have talked the life is too short but if the life is unhappy, we'll tell the life is too long.

We couldn't meet and hear your father in anywhere ever since because of his disappearance. And also we didn't know where they live your sister, Sun-Mi and Sun-Yung. As it were, if the familyhead had a good manner of his family, the family members would be happy. . . .

But, what's the use of talking about the stories? I have no regrets about my vanished youth and I'd like to think that all the things are mine.

I'm sixty years old.

I'm ashamed that I couldn't take care of you earlier. I have not something to tell you about that. My old dreams had been very pleasant, but this reality was far from pleasant. I want to explain my hard life but you won't understand me and my bitter experiences. How reproachable mother I am! I feel like crying to reproach myself endlessly and if you want, I wish to see you in my life. To image your lovely face, this is my only hope.

By and by I live on hope to see you and I wish you success, good luck and your health.

I'll look forward to seeing you and I'll finish my word. Bye.

Yours truly,

Your mother in Seoul.

P.S: I'm so sorry to too late. I can't write in English. So I requested this letter to someone.

弐

> *To him that overcometh, to him will I give of the hidden*
> *manna, and I will give him a white stone, and upon the*
> *stone a new name written, which no one knoweth but he*
> *that receiveth it.*

[REVELATION 2:17]

The beloved queen lay dying. No one could cure her. Frightened whispers swirled like ghosts as day after day the queen lay still, and only her most faithful servants were allowed to enter her rooms.

In desperation, the king called upon two Buddhist monks. They took the pale queen to their hermitage, where they tied one end of a long string around the queen's tumor, the other to a tree outside. The monks chanted, keeping vigil throughout the night. In the morning, the tumor had disappeared: the tree was withered.

Out of gratitude for this miracle, the king helped the monks expand their small hermitage. Eighteen buildings were harmoniously arranged upon their mountain, where they continued to study the philosophy of Flower Garland at the temple named *Haeinsa*, Reflection on a Calm Sea.

Nearly twelve hundred years later, I am resting in the courtyard at Haeinsa. The original hermitage once stood on this site, and it is here that the tree took the illness from the queen.

The spiritual descendants of the two monks go about their daily business at the temple: sitting, studying, chanting. With their shaved heads and loose gray clothing, they are identical to those who have lived and worked here since the seventh century.

Mountains, temples, ancient dolmens: I am afloat in the beauty of a culture deeply mysterious to me and, yet, my birthright. This is the heart of my ancestry, with its dark odor of incense; its rhythmic *tok, tok, tok* of tiny drums; its eighty-four thousand woodblocks containing the Korean Tripitaka, over seven hundred fifty years old and without error, each character carved following one bow to the Buddha.

I must take something from this place, something more meaningful than the plastic tapes of chants, the cheap postcards, the wooden bead bracelets. I must remember what I feel on this day, in this place that swallows me in profuse, deafening color.

I squat to the ground. A small white stone the size of my palm lies next to my feet. It is jagged and dusty, so I wrap it inside a blue handkerchief and place it in my backpack.

I will remember this place, this moment—the blossoming trees, the upturned tile roofs, the way the sun warms my neck—and who I am in this place:

My name is Jeong Kyong-Ah. My family register states the date of my birth, the lunar date January 24, 1972. I am the fifth daughter of Jeong Ho-Joon and the third daughter and fourth child of his second wife, Kang Ahn-Sun. I am the granddaughter of my father's parents, Jeong Song-Pil and Yi Chin-Hwa. I am the granddaughter of my mother's parents, Kang Soon-Ok and Pak Ok-Poon. My ancestry includes landowners, scholars, and government officials. I have six siblings. I am a citizen of the Republic of Korea. I come from a land of pear fields and streams, where Buddhist temples are hidden in the mountains, where people laugh loudly and honor their dead.

Halfway around the world, I am someone else.

I am Jane Marie Brauer, created September 26, 1972, when I was carried off an airplane onto American soil. My State of Minnesota birth certificate declares my date of birth to be March 8, 1972. I am the younger daughter of Frederick and Margaret Brauer. I am the granddaughter of my father's parents, Darwin and Doris Brauer. I am the granddaughter of my mother's parents, Iver and Lourine Reichmann. My ancestors were farmers, factory workers, a sometime Bible salesman. I have one sister; she is my blood sister, adopted with me. I became an American citizen at age five, when I stood before a judge and pledged allegiance to the flag of the United States of America. I come from a land of plains, where the sky touches the earth in uninterrupted horizon, where Lutheran churches dot the corn fields, where stoicism is stamped into the bones of each generation.

In Minnesota, it is night, and Jane Brauer is missing. She is gone—only a memory in the minds of those who imagine her. Meanwhile, in the mountains of Korea, Jeong Kyong-Ah fills her pockets with stones and blinks hard in the sunlight, as if awakened from a deep sleep, or perhaps a very long fugue.

Highway 10

A Play for Imagining

CHARACTERS

FRED, *Caucasian husband of* MARGARET *and father
of* CAROL *and* JANE

MARGARET, *mother of* CAROL *and* JANE, *also Caucasian*

CAROL, *Korean birth sister and adopted sister of* JANE,
4½ years old

JANE, *Korean birth sister and adopted sister of* CAROL,
6 months old

Minnesota, early 1970s. Characters are dressed in middle-class, inexpensive clothing according to the era.

The action on stage must start ten minutes later than advertised on tickets, publicity, and programs. However, houselights must be turned down at scheduled performance time, so that the audience will wait for ten minutes in anticipation. Meanwhile, the sound system plays airport noises—constant talking, public announcements, airplanes taking off and landing. After the action begins, all theater exits must be locked, preventing anyone from leaving before the end of the play. The scene takes place in real time, approximately four hours, or long enough to make the audience feel uncomfortable and trapped.

Night on a rural highway. Fade out airport noises. Fade in sounds of an AM country-western music and weather station. Lights come up slowly on a late 1960s–model American car. The car's passenger side faces out, so the audience views its occupants in profile. Headlights shine full power, giving the impression that the driver, FRED, is able to see only straight ahead. MARGARET sits in the passenger seat holding JANE, and CAROL sits in the seat behind MARGARET, staring out the window into the blackness. During the dialogue, CAROL looks into the audience, examining each person with very large eyes and an expressionless mouth. FRED drives for several minutes, smoking. Sound of a passing car is heard, and its headlights flash across the stage.

FRED:

[*Looks into rearview mirror to see* CAROL] How you doin' back there?

[CAROL *continues to scan the audience*]

MARGARET:

[*Pats baby gently but constantly, like a nervous tic. Turns head to look at* CAROL *but is unable to see her. Speaks over her shoulder.*] Are you okay?

[*Long pause*]

FRED:

[*Louder*] Your mother asked you a question.

[CAROL *does not look at* MARGARET *but searches the faces in the audience, looking for a Korean face, any Korean face. Finding none, she closes her eyes and decides to forget.*]

[*Behind and above the car, fade in a reel-to-reel home movie playing scenes from* CAROL's *(Mi-Ja's) life in Korea. Each scene in Korean language plays for fewer than five seconds before it is faded into black and the next scene plays. Scenes are various memories, showing an account of her young life so far. They include playing with her sisters and friends; eating with her family; sleeping next to her mother; her father raising his fist; a small room; rides on the bus in Seoul; the beginning of her long journey from Kimpo Airport, where she said good-bye to her mother, her uncle, and her elder sisters. At the end of the movie sequence, the Korean memories are completely erased, and the reel-to-reel projector shows blank frames and white noise, as seen at a beginning or ending take-up length of tape.* CAROL *has willed herself to become a girl with no history and is now ready to start her new life.*

The family drives down the highway, the movie projector above them showing nothing but illuminated scratches and other imperfections.]

Harlow, Minnesota, is the Turkey Capital of the World. In Lions Park, Big Tom lords over his habitat. The giant fiberglass turkey faces Town Lake and "downtown" Harlow, which stretches three blocks north to south and two blocks the other way. A butcher shop, bakery, barbershop, and gas station occupy permanent spots in the town's economy, but other businesses come and go. The restaurant used to be the drug store; the store across from the sign advertising "Anteeks" has been transformed from bar to ice cream parlor to furniture store. Swift's, the turkey-processing plant, has closed.

The look of the town changes as utilitarian white letters nailed to storefronts evolve to trendy purple and pink color schemes, but the people remain the same: Americans, mostly of German or Scandinavian descent, who believe in the value of typing, home economics, and machine shop as academic courses and Future Farmers of America for extracurricular enrichment. In August they celebrate Turkey Days, when Miss Harlow, a high school graduate, is crowned on a Friday night after winning the hearts of celebrity judges like Princess Kay of the Milky Way, whose likeness is sculpted into a giant block of butter at the state fair. During the weekend, Miss Harlow presides over the flea market, parade, and demolition derby, all in an evening gown and tiara. Because everyone deserves a chance, the contestant who knows she will win neither the crown nor the competitions in talent, swimsuit, evening gown, or interview can always work hard to be nice and earn the title of Miss Congeniality.

In Harlow, men must be husbands and fathers. If they are not, they are eccentric old bachelor cousins or junior high English teachers.

Likewise, women are wives and mothers. They must be mothers, not just wives, and if the children are not born soon, people talk. They ask nice questions. These in turn became questions my mother asked herself: When are you going to have children? What is a woman without a family? After years of marriage, collecting toys for children, and mothering cats and dogs, those same questions became twisted in her mind: Why hadn't God chosen to bless her and her husband with a family? What was wrong with her body? What was wrong with her husband's body?

Mom and Dad had nieces and nephews to visit, but the hallway in their own house was devoid of pictures. The bedrooms were empty, the rec room downstairs quiet. There were no diapers to change, no birthday parties to plan, no homework to supervise.

But there was church to attend every Sunday, and depending on who died or got married, Mom and Dad could also attend on Saturdays or maybe Wednesdays. There was work to do, ways to feel useful. Dad wouldn't read the lessons because he wasn't a good speaker, but he would usher, silently nodding the parishioners in and out of their pews, collecting offerings, standing at the front of church so that the pastor could bless the wooden plates. He'd never angle for a board position, and Mom would never try for a secretarial position; they were too humble for that. But they could wash pews, make hotdishes and bars, serve dinners, prepare for another baby's baptism. They could help kids make plaques out of beans and alphabet noodles, show how an X turned sideways became the cross, where Jesus X'd out our sins. At the end of Maple Street, Bethlehem Lutheran Church of the Missouri Synod was always a welcoming place, a place to feel needed.

Each member of the congregation was bound to act in community, with one mission, and all those working hands and offerings added up. Those hands and dollars, multiplied by one hundred fifty-seven Lutheran congregations across Minnesota, equaled Lutheran Social Service.

Lutheran Social Service was for changing lives.

Every week, Pastor Mattson saw the empty spot in the pew beside Mom and Dad, where there should have been a growing family. Shaking Mom's hand while leaning forward to whisper into her ear one Sunday, Pastor asked if he could meet with them in his office after coffee hour. Mom couldn't imagine why.

They thought maybe their offerings weren't large enough or maybe they were not involved enough. But Pastor, who had changed into a dark suit, shook their hands, touched their shoulders, and seated them opposite his enormous desk, the sun throwing harsh, examining light through the modern sixties windows that did not open.

"Mr. and Mrs. Brauer," he began. "It has come to my attention that there are some children who need you."

If it were possible, I would move back to Harlow. But I have been living in the city for twelve years, and it would be hard to say good-bye to United Noodles grocery store and Dr. Wong, who still can't get my name right but who can cure me with acupuncture. I prefer *kimchi* to sauerkraut these days, and I eat turkey only for Thanksgiving.

If I were from Harlow, I would never have left in the first place.

Harlow is the last bastion of all that is good, right, fundamental, and homogenous. It's the kind of place where vandalism to a flower garden makes front-page news, where the weather has an effect on what you wear and hunt, where all the people celebrate the same holidays, where you don't have to remember the latest politically correct vocabulary.

Harlow has its own self-purging system. The Hmong people came and left. There is no gay/lesbian/bi/transgender support group. The sole black person of Harlow, adopted and raised by a white family, punched in his years as a high school drumming phenomenon, lived through rumors that he raped his adoptive sister, then left and never came back. It's not that the Nicaraguan refugee family or anyone else was chased out of town by a torch-wielding posse. The homogeneity is probably more due to the fact that the minorities who've been brought in by church groups eventually figure out where to move to be among their own. And then they leave.

But for those who are already home, it's a good place to raise children. And why not raise them just the way you were raised? Maybe raise them even better.

Mom taught me the elements of embroidery and macramé; Dad taught me the names of all the trees on our forty acres. He taught me which kinds crackle in the fire, which kinds burn slowly through the night. Life on Mears Lake was filled with small pleasures—fresh wild strawberries; blackened shoes on newspaper; the lake's turnover in spring and fall; the lowing of cows on the opposite side of the bay; the unblinking eyes of sunfish at the bottom of the boat.

⤳

My Korean mother's face is luminous. She sits in the center of the black-and-white portrait with my father. She wears her traditional *hanbok* and holds me, her baby, in her arms. My father wears a dark suit. Behind them, two daughters stand in school blazers, and two more small daughters in hanboks flank the parents on either side. They are solemn, not smiling for this formal family portrait.

My kindergarten class was fascinated by the photograph.

"Is that really you?" they chimed.

"Yes," I said, "and this is my Korean family."

"What else do you have to show us today?" prodded Mrs. Hoffman.

"I would like to show the boys and girls real Korean clothes," I announced, reaching into my paper grocery bag.

"Can you tell us more about your clothes?" Mrs. Hoffman's whipped-up brown hair was like cotton candy. She smelled like Cashmere Bouquet. I was in love with her.

"Um," I stalled, not knowing anything about Korean clothing or traditions. Then I remembered my one fact, my single piece of Korean history. "My mother sent them to me when I was a baby, after I came to America. It's a Christmas present."

"Thank you very much, Jane," said Mrs. Hoffman. "Now, boys and girls, be very, very careful when you pass Jane's picture and clothes around. These things cannot be replaced. Be very careful."

The items made their way around the circle, each child *oooh*-ing and *aaah*-ing over the beautiful embroidery, the rainbow-colored sleeves, and the strange rubber shoes, shaped like Indian canoes.

"And now," said Mrs. Hoffman, "Jane and I will leave you with Miss Benson while we show and tell for Mrs. Evans's class. Jane's show and tell is very special because we don't often get to see things from other countries. Everyone is on their best behavior now. Let's go, Jane."

In Mrs. Evans's kindergarten class, we repeated the same show and tell to more wonderment from children and adults. My heart swelled up like a shiny red balloon; never before had I been singled out for such special attention. Two teachers, two teacher's aides, and thirty-two children all noticed me that day and how special I was just for being me. I rode the bus home nearly bursting with pride.

My mommy loves me a lot. She lets me sit on her lap in the rocking chair after school, even though I'm too big for that. I am holding the photograph, telling her what a good day it was at school today. I hold the picture by its frame, and then it occurs to me to look at my face more closely, to see if what Carol had told me was true: that we were given away because I was too ugly. I examine the face for a deformity. Is the mouth too large? Are the eyes too small? Do I really look like a frog?

I think I don't look that bad. I look like a regular baby. So Carol can't be right. There must be a different reason why we were given away. But why would anyone give away her children? Don't all mommies love their babies?

My forehead scrunches up, and I feel something like a burn rise up out of my chest and into my throat, behind the jaw, making my chin quiver, behind the nose and into the eyes, and I start to drip.

"Why did she give us away?" I ask my mommy, my little mouth curved into a tipped crescent moon, show-and-tell triumph somehow twisted into a wet question mark.

The rocking stops. She stands up swiftly, like a reflex, shedding me from her lap. I wait, thinking she will come back.

In my memory, twenty-five years later, I search through the house for my mom. I listen for clattering in the kitchen. Nothing. I listen for the click of her shoes against the linoleum. Silence. In my memory, I rise from the chair, and I look downstairs. No one. No one in the bedrooms. The house is empty.

She seems to have evaporated.

In my memory, I am alone in the still rocking chair. Outside, it is autumn. The oak leaves are red. The poplar leaves are yellow. The clouds are white.

She does not return.

I know I've made my mommy angry. I want to run and say I'm sorry, I'm sorry, I'm sorry, I'm sorry I made you mad, I won't ask again. But the house is empty. Who will listen to my words? Who will forgive me? I'm left alone in the rocking chair, legs too short to touch the floor, legs too short to make the chair rock. Who could love such a stupid child who says such stupid things? There must be something wrong with me. I must be rotten, truly bad. Carol must be right.

"We chose you," my mommy always says. To me that means from a store, because when you go to the store you look at the rows of dolls and you choose. A thought comes to me now, a frightening thought that makes sense as I sit alone: I could also be returned to the store. I could be exchanged for a better girl, someone who thinks better and who doesn't say hurtful things. No, I don't want to be returned. I want to stay here, because I love my family, and because if two mothers gave me away, certainly no one would ever, *ever* want me again. Then I would have to live in the store forever.

I don't want to be alone in a big dark store at night, like Corduroy the bear, who lost his button. I don't want to sit on a shelf with rows and rows of other girls, and where would we all sleep at night, and who would tuck us in?

I must be very, very good so my mommy will keep me. I won't ask any more stupid questions. I won't do anything to make her mad.

I will be so good for her.

I will be perfect.

Pastor Mattson produced a thin brochure from behind his desk. "Every Child is Precious in His Sight," he read out loud. He opened the brochure to a photograph of a forlorn Korean girl. He looked right into Mom's eyes, then into Dad's.

"These children could have been aborted, but their mothers chose life for them. Often the mothers are prostitutes or teenagers, and they cannot take care of their own children. But these babies need homes and parents who love them, and they need to be brought up in the love of Jesus Christ our Savior. It is the work of the Holy Spirit through our church that God has blessed us with the opportunity to help these children in need."

"Well," Dad began, "we would certainly like a family."

"But from overseas?" Mom asked.

"God does not see the color of our skin," said Pastor. "He made us all the same in His image. He sees only souls. Open your heart to Jesus's love for all his little children. Let Him work His miracles through you."

Mom and Dad went home and discussed the brochure that Pastor gave them. There was something strange about the thought of adopting from Korea, but adoption did seem like a plausible choice. Maybe they should call the agency and see about adopting a Caucasian American child. A boy if possible—an infant. But there were no white boys available.

They read the brochure again:

Lutheran Adoption Service focuses on both the child and prospective parent. They believe every child has a right to permanent parents who can provide an atmosphere of love, acceptance, and supportive care. Each child should have the security of family life experience, the opportunity to grow in Christian faith, and to develop his special endowment. They also believe married couples who desire to share of themselves in helping a child should have the opportunity to experience the satisfactions and responsibilities of parenthood.

Yes, they did want to help a child. Yes, they did want to give a child a home. Yes, they wanted to give a child the opportunity to grow in Christian faith.

They endured the home study: God had not seen fit to give them their own child, but if they could prove to the social worker from Moorhead that they were good enough, earned enough, were Christian enough—then they might get a baby another way.

The call finally came, two years later: there was an older girl, already four and a half years old, who spoke no English. But she seemed bright, played well, liked to sing. She was hard to place because she was older than most parents wanted, but she came with a baby sister. Would they adopt siblings?

Yes, they wanted to be parents.

B R E A D

Dissolve:

2 packages yeast   1 c. water

Melt together:

1 quart milk   2 T. salt

6 T. sugar   1/4 c. Crisco

Mix in:

10 c. flour

Let rise twice. Bake 30 min. Makes 4 loaves.

Mom's bread recipe, the same as her mother's and her mother's, was good. It was, in fact, very good. But she didn't submit it or anything else to the town cookbook; humility kept her from crowing all over town about her bread. When the town cookbook came out a year later, she bought three copies, and indeed so-and-so of the turkey-growing family and so-and-so of the truck-line family were in that cookbook between recipes for hard soap and pickled crab apples, with their fancy, expensive-ingredient recipes, bragging about how they got the idea for butterscotch and chocolate chips in the same cookie from their friend in Denver, who sold them for *thirty-nine cents* each. Mom kept her recipes to herself and nursed a secret and unborn dream of opening a catering business from inside her own kitchen, and people would talk about her and compliment her en masse for her potato salad, her chocolate-chip cookies, and her very good bread.

In this dream—which was always just a dream—nothing could go wrong. The potato salad was always tangy, the bottoms of cookies would never burn, the bread would never catch a draft and sit stubborn in its pan, flat as a communion wafer.

When Mom dreamed of having babies, she bought a toy bear at Crazy Daze Sidewalk Sale to hold the place of the child. When I was old enough to claim that bear for my own, I called him Jimmy until I decided he should be renamed Mary and dressed him in different clothes. Explanation: Mary was the twin sister of Jimmy, but Jimmy had died, and he was buried in the ground far away, same as my father's elder brother who died as a baby and was buried underneath a stone lamb somewhere near Lansing, Michigan, a place my father had never visited.

That baby must have been a ghost around my dad's head. The promise of a life is always rosier than the actualization of it; the nonexistent can do nothing wrong.

Years after Mary Bear was boxed away, Grandma Reichmann died, and I finally learned her real name: Lourine. I panicked when I saw it on the funeral cards because I thought the printer had made a mistake: I always thought her name was Lorraine.

Lourine's children were taught not to cross their father, and they learned the unspoken things by observing the space around them, as an artist draws the negative space around a chair or bowl of apples. So when Grandpa addressed his second wife with the name of his first wife, Lorraine, all the kids knew why and ignored it. And the grandkids never knew her real name until she died.

First wife Lorraine and Grandpa had divorced after only a couple years of marriage. In his memory, she would always be a pretty, young bride.

When my mom married my dad at age eighteen, she inherited this ill-fitting, shimmering crown of expectation, perhaps not to wear herself but to pass on to us, her daughters, who would be haunted by the birth child who was never conceived, this pink-skinned boy who had pretty blue eyes like his mother and a funny smile like his father. We would be haunted by this shadow and by the ghosts of our own dead twins, whom we had simply replaced one day by changing clothes: Kyong-Ah, who lived to the age of six months, and Mi-Ja, who died at four years of age when she became Carol. From the photographic evidence, Carol came into this world as a child and was never a baby at all.

Because I was a baby, I was appropriately cuddly and showed affection to all the right people at all the right times. The few problems that arose were easily handled: temper tantrums would dissolve if ignored; chronic morning tummy aches could be soothed with candy mints; an unwillingness to sleep could be cured by the sound of the vacuum cleaner or a ride in the car.

Carol also assimilated well, just as Mom and Dad were promised she would. Her behavior was polite, clean, and not wasteful: she would dive underneath the table to retrieve a single grain of rice if one fell to the floor. Getting her to understand the importance of a regular bedtime was a more difficult matter, but overindulging her solved the problem: late at night, she was allowed to watch television, straight-backed, cross-legged, and centered in the middle of the living room floor. After that she was more than happy to go to bed at a decent hour.

According to Mom, Carol spoke one Korean word repeatedly and for no visible reason. Mom matched it up on the vocabulary list provided by Lutheran Social Service: *apum,* pain. Other than that, Carol didn't even try to speak until the day complete English sentences came out of her just like anyone else. By the time she enrolled in kindergarten, less than a year later, there were only a few words she could not pronounce, among them "buffalo." Her hilarious rendition: *bupparo*.

She remembered one Korean word, apparently, and one Korean song: in Mom and Dad's first family photo album, between pictures of our dual baptism, there is a photograph of Carol singing this song, the same one captured on a reel-to-reel recorder by our teenaged cousin. Carol's eyes are shut, her mouth open in melody, an expression like rapture on her face. But she is silent, the note caught behind her front teeth like an unpeeled orange, in stasis, before the end of the exhalation.

It must have been a character flaw—not her mother's ignorance of a Korean body or a child's way of behaving that worked in her past life but was inapplicable in her new life—that made her remote, made her scrub her skin until it turned red, gave her frequent nosebleeds right before the school bus came, and made her so independent that Mom had to hug her by force, holding her arms down and squeezing her tight. Frustrated, Dad asked her, "Do you know why we love Jane more?"

"We love Jane more" is all Carol heard, and this girl who was sacrificed by her Umma to save her baby sister grew to resent me, resent the original command from Umma to take care of me, resent the care-giving commands Mom gave her as she grew into a pre-teen and wanted to have her own life, her own age-appropriate interests, unencumbered by babysitting and playing. So although I simply adored her, loved her with every part of my being, worshipped her and her hairstyles as only a little sister can, she was happy to be at college two hundred fifty miles away by the time I entered ninth grade.

And that whole time we never spoke a single word to each other about Korea. We wove a gag over our mouths as thick and impenetrable as love.

Ma: *Feeling different again, huh?*

Navin: *It's like I don't fit in. It's like I don't belong here.*

Ma: *It's your birthday and it's time you knew.*
Navin, you're not our natural-born child.

Navin: *I'm not?*

Ma: *You were left on our doorstep but we raised you
like you were one of us.*

Navin: *You mean I'm going to stay this color?*

[STEVE MARTIN AND CARL GOTTLIEB, THE JERK]

The Ice House Restaurant

A Musical

CHARACTERS
FRED, *Caucasian husband and father*
MARGARET, *Caucasian wife and mother*
CAROL, *Korean, sixth grade*
JANE, *Korean, second grade*
WAITRESS, *middle-aged, a career waitress*
CHORUS OF DINERS, *Caucasian, rural Minnesotans
of all ages*

*The action of the play takes place in a rural Minnesota eatery named
"The Ice House Restaurant" for its location on Big Lake Clara, where
men chopped ice for use in iceboxes until the mid 1940s. Huge black ice
tongs and photographs of wagons loaded with lake ice and straw are
mounted on the walls.*

Characters are dressed in inexpensive clothing of the early 1980s.

*Begin piano background music: Hank Williams favorites. Lights up on
an empty table in the middle of the restaurant. The restaurant is filled with
DINERS sitting at the tables in the perimeter. Sounds of eating, talking,
clattering of dishes. FAMILY enters and removes coats at the coat rack.
When the characters at the other tables see the FAMILY, they stop eating,*

put their heads together, whisper, and point with butter knives. When the FAMILY *is seated, action resumes around them as normal.*

WAITRESS:

[*Brings menus and water in four red plastic glasses*] How are you folks tonight? Tonight our soup is creamy chicken and wild rice, and the special is fried walleye pike with baked potato, and your choice of carrot coins or french beans. That comes with a roll and the salad bar. Can I get you any drinks or appetizers?

FRED:

Ah, what the heck. I'll have an Old Mil.

WAITRESS:

Can I get anything for you?

MARGARET:

I'll have a Southern Comfort Manhattan, please.

WAITRESS:

Real good then. Anything for you girls?

CAROL AND JANE:

[*Shake their heads signaling no*]

WAITRESS:

Alrighty, folks, I'll be back in just a minute with your drinks. [*Exit*]

[FAMILY *looks at menus*]

MARGARET:

I'm hungry for a steak tonight. What are you having, Fred?

FRED:

That special sounded pretty good to me. I wonder what's on that salad bar.

JANE:

[*to* MARGARET] That man is looking at me.

MARGARET:

Who?

JANE:

That one over there. [*Tilts her head in his direction*] Why are people always looking at us?

MARGARET:

Nobody's looking at you.

JANE:

[*Shoots the man a dirty look and continues to read menu*]

[*Music crescendos and accelerates. Adult* DINERS *individually rush the* FAMILY's *table, forming a crowd. Shouts are audible over the chorus: "What cute little girls you have! Do they speak Chinese? How big will they get? What pretty almond eyes! Look at the tiny waists! Feel their hair! It's so thick!" Some of the* DINERS *touch the girls as if they are dolls and push* CAROL *and* JANE *roughly in their chairs.* MARGARET *and* FRED *continue reading their menus, holding them over their faces, oblivious to the crowd of* DINERS *at their table. Finally all* DINERS *in the restaurant are crowded around the table, pushing* CAROL *and* JANE *back and forth and shouting randomly.*]

DINERS:

Rice-picker! I don't want my kids to play with those girls. Go back to where you came from. Can they speak English? Roses are red, violets are bigger, you got the lips of an African nigger! Do you need extra help in school? Would you like to adopt this stray dog we found? All you people are good at math. Frog-eyed chink! Boat person! How much did they cost? Where did you get them? Chinese, Japanese, dirty knees, look at these! Don't you understand me? It's so kind of you to have foster children. Would you be interested in some foreign exchange students? Can they use chopsticks? What do they eat? Where did you learn to speak English so well? I know someone who adopted Korean girls. Do you know them? Gook!

[DINERS *continue to push and shout while the stage lights dim to black.* CAROL *and* JANE *bite down hard on their lower lips. Pianist vamps out on "Hey, Good Lookin'."*]

American girls like basically the same things, including but not limited to unicorns, fun clothes, baby animals, stories about princesses, music with a good beat, stickers, and butterflies. So, when Miss Larson announced that the class science project would be to raise monarch butterflies, at least half the class was thrilled, and the other half was a spectrum ranging from almost thrilled to indifferent to belligerent. The most suave of the boys, the pack leader whose dad was the gym teacher, expressed his opinion of the project by wrapping his feet around the back legs of his desk chair, tipping backwards against the wall, and taking another bite out of his Chapstick.

"But before we raise the monarch butterflies, we must first complete a written assignment," said Miss Larson, the architect of incentives like spelling dollars and math cart, a career teacher who always made sure her students learned properly and thoroughly.

Although she must have been in her fifties, "she never married." People said this with a knowing nod, as if she were a Miss Havisham who had been tragically jilted. According to Harlow legend, one morning during church coffee hour, when Miss Larson was again standing conspicuously by herself, Mrs. Graham, the town gossip, confronted her and actually said, right to her face, "Miss Larson, when are you going to get married and have a family?"

And Miss Larson replied with a laugh, "What do I need children for? I have all my students."

Mrs. Graham laughed with her, but at the ladies aide meeting afterwards, Mrs. Graham clutched her Styrofoam coffee cup with its lipstick imprints and announced to the shocked ladies that Miss Larson did not intend to find a husband and have a family.

They prayed for her.

But despite the prayers of the ladies aide and all of their friends and all of *their* friends, Miss Larson remained a Miss, not a Mrs., for many years, until finally her marital status was accepted as fixed. Anyone who didn't know the story would be told, "You see, her *students* are her children," and an enlightened "oh" or "you don't say" would escape the listener's lips as the equation of a woman with no children was finally understood.

Although the moms and dads of Harlow felt sorry for Miss Larson, that poor old woman who lived in an upstairs apartment in town, they also knew she was a good teacher, and they wanted their children to benefit from her spinsterhood. While other teachers spent evenings with their families, the people of Harlow knew that Miss Larson spent her evenings alone, grading papers, assembling bulletin boards, and dreaming up wonderful projects like raising monarch butterflies.

My teacher was the stuff of legend, and I knew that Mom and Dad had specifically requested—to the principal, no less—that I be assigned to her fourth grade class. I liked Miss Larson and her pinky-beigeness. She wasn't the kind of teacher to give hugs or hover too close over your shoulder, but there was something lovely and refined about her uniforms of pink blouses, khaki skirts, and beige nurse's shoes. Her neck and head were a natural continuation of her color scheme; she reminded me of a baby condor with bits of nest stuck to its head.

"Mr. Anderson! Four on the floor!" Miss Larson commanded my Chapstick-eating classmate, and he rolled his eyes and put his chair back into a neutral position. "As I was saying, we must first complete a written assignment."

"Migration." Miss Larson wrote the word on the board and underlined it twice for emphasis. "Monarch butterflies migrate every year from Minnesota to Mexico and back again. We will spend the next three weeks studying the life cycle of the monarch." She continued to explain, using laminated pictures and her world map, which she dramatically unrolled right over "Migration." The girls couldn't wait to write their reports.

A butterfly is cute as a diamond. Monarch butterflies are orange and black.

This is how you raise them.

1. Find milkweed with monarch eggs on it.
2. Put a dry paper towel in the bottom of a glass jar.
3. Put the milkweed and a twig in the jar.
4. Close the jar with a piece of nylon and a rubber band.
5. Change the leaves every day.
6. The eggs turn into a caterpillar.
7. The caterpillar turns into a chrysalis.
8. The chrysalis turns into a butterfly.

Monarchs migrate. This is different than species that emigrate. Species that emigrate only travel one way. Species that migrate travel back and forth between two different places. They have two homes.

Monarch butterflies migrate south in August. They fly to California or Mexico. A butterfly can fly 3,000 miles. It is a very long journey. Sometimes they have to stop drinking so the water in their bodies won't freeze. They stay together to try to stay warm. After they fly so far, their wings are torn and ragged. It is a miracle that they can fly so far.

It takes generations of butterflies to complete the migration cycle. The butterflies returning to Mexico or California every fall are the great-great-grandchildren of those who left the previous spring. No one knows how they can find their way.

Dear Mother,

Today is my birthday. Are you thinking of me? I think of you every year on my birthday. Do you remember when I was born? I have been making letters and pictures for you. Pretty soon I will have a whole boxful. My mommy says I can give them to you when I die someday. When we meet, you can tell me about yourself. What is your favorite color? What do you like to eat? I will find out if the storybooks I made about you are true. Until then, I will keep these letters and pictures I drew in a safe place. I can't wait for the day that we meet in Heaven.

Love,
Jane

"What does it feel like to not know your real mom?"

My classmates were genuinely puzzled. My answer was meant to be both caustic and self-protective: "What does it feel like to *know* your real mom?"

I did not know how to explain to them, "It feels awful. Weird. It feels like I was never born. I want to know what you feel like, when you look at your family and people look like you. I want to know what you feel like when you're at your grandparents' house, and they haul out the box of family photos, and all the aunts and uncles talk and laugh about how you're the carrier of the family nose or the family eyes, or how you look just like your aunt when she was your age. What does *that* feel like? What does it feel like when you hug your mother, and you're just the right size so that your face comes up to her belly, where you came from? What does it feel like to pass a mirror and *not be surprised?*"

The a-word, adoption, was not mentioned in our house. Neither was the K-word, Korea. There were no books about adopted children, no celebrations of adoption day or naturalization day, no culture camps to attend. They raised us the way they were supposed to—like we were their own.

But there were clues, things that my mom held on to for at least a little while.

There was a letter. I found it one day in my mom's desk, in a red, white, and blue airmail envelope, the very light kind that you can see through. There was a return address. I copied it and began to send letters to my mother in Korea.

When I remember those maudlin letters now, I am embarrassed. It couldn't have been that bad. Still, I do not know for what reason a child would spend so much time writing lies. These letters were my private way of grieving, of crying to my mythical mother, because my parents here would not listen, would not see. So I wrote and wrote, in childish print on Garfield stationery, and sent the messages out into the world with a wish that, somewhere, the letters would find eyes to read them, a heart to hear.

They went out. They didn't come back. Or maybe they did, with a purple stamp in the shape of a pointing hand: "Return to Sender. Address Unknown." But this I don't know: my mom got the mail every day before I came home from school.

Carol had come to America malnourished and, therefore, legally blind. A steady diet of American food and all the Minute Rice she could eat gradually healed her eyesight, and the cat's-eye, Coke-bottle glasses grew thinner and less ridiculous every year. My eyes, however, started out fine and then gave up in second grade, at which point the eye doctor issued me red, buglike glasses and assigned me various eye-focusing exercises. After my eyes' initial failing, the optometrist bravely and biannually tried to save my sight from complete deterioration.

During one of those afternoons in the waiting room, I read a story from a thick, aquamarine book that had been disguised in the shuffle of *Highlights* magazines and *Ladies' Home Journals*. It was about a girl in unbearable pain—leprosy, the pox, boils, something like that. Her despairing mother appealed to the Lord for intervention. He sent a prophet, who commanded the mother to hold the diseased girl's hands over her head from sundown to sunrise, so God might see her and pity her and so bring her to paradise where she would join all those who had gone before her. God was indeed merciful, and He did grant wishes. He saw her, and the little girl died before sunrise.

MISS LARSON'S FACE WAS ALSO DEFINED BY GLASSES, perched atop her beaky nose. So I felt an affinity toward her, which she reciprocated by finding me a friend in Korea.

My pen pal was the daughter of an American missionary from

Tennessee, a friend of a friend of Miss Larson's. Her father's assignment was Daejeon, a city nowhere near my birthplace, but in my mind Korea was about as big as my hometown, and of course all Koreans knew each other. Holly's life seemed almost the same as mine—she went to American school, had American friends, wore American clothes. She sent me a picture of her cat—black with white socks. I sent her long, overly detailed letters covered in stickers. And I ended every letter with a request: Would she please find my mother? Of course, she was not going to walk down the street, knock on a door, and identify my mother, but what did I know?

AS MY WORLD BEGAN TO GROW, I learned how things worked: I discovered the miracle of transformation. I suffered through long division: neat answers materialized on top of brackets; the remainders tidied themselves up after a capital letter "R." I read "Fog" by Carl Sandburg, a poem that transforms an everyday event in seven words: "The fog comes / on little cat feet." I performed experiments with potatoes and litmus paper. I started piano lessons and learned that the mysterious marks on the page can be lifted, invisibly, into the same air that you breathe, where they become music.

I went to a funeral at a Catholic church, complete with stained glass windows and blasphemous icons. The martyrs and disciples hovered on this side of life, despite arrows and nails hanging out of their bodies, and the Madonna statue managed to look happy and sad at the same time. The hocus-pocus, incense-swinging priest (who didn't even know the end of the Lord's Prayer) seemed more credible than the pastor at my Lutheran church, whose sermons on the Gospels always made some very tenuous connection to the Minnesota Vikings. And although Martin Luther decreed that I must wait to take communion until eighth grade, even small children could take Catholic communion, and Catholic bread and wine literally become the body and blood of Christ the moment they hit your stomach. The people from the church down the street had tapped into something magical. Compared to the somber, icon-shunning, bare-pine-bench-sitting Lutherans, Catholics had more fun.

Magic existed. If Jesus could be born out of wedlock and I hadn't really been born at all—but was still here—I could count on magic to get some other things done.

HAVING MADE MY WAY THROUGH all the horse and dog books at the library, I started to read books about the paranormal. I was on the lookout for poltergeists, ghosts, and aliens; my sister and I conducted ESP experiments which were at least fifty percent successful, thanks to my gullibility when she confirmed that yes, she did get the telepathic message, and yes, that was the color she was thinking of, too.

Since the mailman was not doing the best job delivering letters to my mother, I thought I could use telepathy to send her a message. But sending a message across the living room was one thing; sending a message across the ocean was another. I needed extra postage.

Carol and I had been pounding rocks to dust since day one. It was a game she had brought with her from Korea—a child with few toys, she played with what was available. So, in the long summer afternoons, we gathered up landscaping rocks and pulverized them on the sidewalk. Shale and chalk rocks were the best for grinding into magic dust. Big pieces of granite broke smaller rocks into chips, and smooth, round rocks ground the little chips into a fine powder. Magic dust, usually bright yellow, could help you fly (à la Peter Pan) if sprinkled on your head; it could be mixed with water and stuck to your legs; it could be used on dolls to help prevent diaper rash.

It made sense that since magic dust was multipurpose, it could also be used to send a message. I gathered up the very best, yellowest chalk rocks from outside the house, retrieved my best grinding stones from the window well, and squatted on the sidewalk, transforming heavy stones into dust that could be airborne. I said what I hoped was a Catholic blessing over the powder. Then I gathered up the dust in my hands and wished hard. I closed my eyes and brought my cupped hands to my face, imbuing the magic dust with my silent message: *Mother, mother, mother. Where are you? Please come for me.* Then, when the message was securely fastened to the dust, I turned my small back to the wind and exhaled. I sent the message to my mother with all my breath, with all my life force. The dust was lifted up for a moment, like a beautiful, golden angel on the wind, and then it settled back onto the lawn.

THAT NIGHT, I SAT IN THE DARK LISTENING to the sporadic laughter of the *Tonight Show* snaking through the hallway and into my bedroom. Johnny Carson staked out his territory in our house every night at ten o'clock; Dad glowed blue in the flicker, silent, watching monkeys and musicians and movie stars.

Mom was in the next room, sewing. I could see the glow of her lamp, hear the hum of her Singer machine, interrupted only by the snap of shears or the tinkle of pins in a dish.

In the twin bed next to mine, Carol was asleep.

Although my unaided eyes could not discern shapes more than two feet in front of them, I could see the neighbor's garage light, a glowing orb not unlike, I thought, the star of Bethlehem. I focused on the light outside my window, far away, the only thing visible. I sat up straight in bed and lifted my arms high above my head.

Ed McMahon chortled. Mom reverse-stitched the end of a hem.

If I die before I wake, I pray the Lord my soul to take. Hands in the air, I thought I might be transformed into the girl in the story, or maybe into one of those happy-sad people in a stained glass window. Nothing happened. Maybe it didn't work for Lutherans. Maybe God couldn't see me through the ceiling. My hands blazed. When I could no longer hold up my arms, I resigned myself to the nightly inevitable.

Sleep came on little cat feet.

The oak leaves and poplar leaves fell, grew, turned red and yellow, fell, grew, turned, fell, and still there was no explanation, no answer to the question posed by my five-year-old self: *Don't all mommies love their babies?* Since then, I have heard explanations from other adopted people's parents: "Your mother loved you very much, but she could not take care of you." Or, "Your mother wanted to give you a better life. She knew that you would have more opportunities here." Or, "I don't know, but you can be sure that she loves you and still thinks about you."

I made up my own explanation, one that made sense to a child. I decided that my mother was a beautiful princess. Something terrible had happened to her (probably involving a dragon), and her children were taken away. I drew pictures of her inside her tower, where she was trapped, so far away from me. Of course she missed me and thought about me constantly.

Later I discovered how close to the truth I was. My mother was not a princess, but she *was* born into a kind of aristocracy. In the traditional Korean class system, my ancestors rose to a high social rank through a combination of strategic marriages, inheritance, moral behavior, and government examinations.

Your mother's parents had many cows. Translators always seem impressed. My family led an easy, country life in what is now the central part of South Korea; they left the backbreaking work of farming to tenants while they enjoyed the privileges of the literati. It was the ideal kind of life for a Korean nobleman: idleness in the countryside, close to nature, the mind free to study *The Analects* of Confucius, to paint, to write *sijo*.

My grandparents would be the last generation to enjoy the aristocratic, scholarly lifestyle. Now their great house with its many buildings, the fine tile roof, the massive pillars, and the open courtyard lies in disrepair, abandoned, empty.

My grandparents raised their family during *Amhukki*. The first decade of Japanese colonial rule is called "the Dark Period" because of the extreme inhumanity and degradation the Korean people suffered.

The residue of the Dark Period remains: the old generation cannot forget the measured brutality inflicted by one Confucian culture upon another, no matter how friendly the politicians on TV act now. And as I become my mother's daughter—as I become Korean again—I feel the anger of my people in ways that are not acceptable to an American living in a pluralistic society. However, as an American (conveniently disregarding the ironies of my own country's policies), I also despise those who take away freedom of religion, speech, and thought, who offer two choices: assimilation or starvation.

One might blame my ancestors for weakening Korea by hoarding power and wealth, making it easy for the Japanese to exploit Korea's peasants even before they occupied her. It is true that there were problems inherent in the class system, yet the *Kabo* reforms, set in motion by the upper class in the late nineteenth century, strove to abolish class distinctions. These reforms never had time to develop, however; the Japanese annexed Korea as a colony in 1910, taking away the Koreans' right to govern themselves.

Many Americans may not know about this time of suffering in Korea's history because in America we focus on American and Western European war history—the Holocaust in particular. And, while in our popular culture there is a fascination with all things Japanese or Chinese, very few people know about the unique culture that lies between those two countries.

Americans are often surprised to learn about the character of the Korean people, who are made of more substance than the one thing they seem to be known for: spicy pickled kimchi. But maybe it was the simple things like traditional food that helped the people endure while their palaces, temples, names, families, and social systems were robbed or destroyed by Japanese occupation. Even now, it could be kimchi that fuels the growth of modern Seoul. A view from the tower on Namsan Mountain reveals skyscrapers packed together in a metropolis as great as New York, a city completely rebuilt less than fifty years after having been burned, shelled, annihilated. And it may be this fire in the belly that nourishes the quiet determination that replaced Buddha's diamond third eye at Seokguram Grotto with a yellow crystal to shine on winter solstice; that faithfully reconstructs palaces from ashes and hundred-year-old photographs; that has finally summoned the courage to demand justice for "comfort women" who, after being either tricked or kidnapped, were forced into sexual slavery for Japanese soldiers and raped up to thirty times a day in the service of the Japanese Empire, until they either died or were left to live with permanent injuries, illnesses, and shame.

Some say that the Japanese royal family is really Korean, because they eat with chopsticks and a spoon, as Koreans do, whereas the common people of Japan eat with only chopsticks. It is also said that perhaps all Japanese are descended from Koreans; the geography makes it seem possible. It is said that a giant bell lies silent at the bottom of the East Sea (Americans call it the Sea of Japan), where it fell from a boat, far from its temple in Korea. And it is rumored that Japan's National Treasure No. 1, the Future Buddha, is stolen from Korea, and that is why it is not often displayed. Perhaps only neighbors and family can be so heartless.

During the occupation, the Japanese sought to destroy Korean cultural and racial consciousness by assimilating the people. Ironically, the assimilation could never be complete because Koreans were never considered equal to Japanese. Even today this attitude persists; third-generation Koreans living in Japan are denied citizenship because of their ancestry.

The subjugation began with the permeation of the government by the Japanese, followed by police control that prescribed everything from religious practices to the slaughter of animals. While Koreans were being shipped to Manchuria to work, the Japanese seized almost forty percent of the land belonging to the late Chosun Dynasty and sold it to their own companies and settlers. Both aristocrats and peasants were made to enlist in the Japanese army; the army was fed on the same rice that was rationed out to the farmers who grew it.

The Japanese knew how to demean the Korean people most effectively. They suppressed the language, requiring schoolchildren to use only Japanese, and literally took away people's Korean names, "graciously allowing" them to adopt Japanese names. They imprisoned people for the crime of compiling a Korean dictionary. Christianity and Buddhism were banned; only the Japanese traditional religion was allowed. People who refused to worship at Shinto shrines were denied ration coupons. The men were forced to cut off their treasured long hair, a most clever humiliation.

Naively inspired by the idealistic fourteen points of Woodrow Wilson—he was thinking about Europe, not Asia, when he championed humanism and respect for self-determination for all people—Koreans organized a massive, peaceful nationalist movement. Completely surprising the Japanese, young and old alike proclaimed independence on March 1, 1919, chanting *Taehan tongnip mansei*, "Long live an independent Korea." It was an exercise in unity and will, sparking a movement that was to last several months. According to a Korean nationalist estimate (the Japanese count is different), 7,500 Koreans were killed, 15,000 injured, and 45,000 arrested between March and December of that year.

The occupation lasted until Japan's surrender at the end of World War II. Strategically important, Korea then became a pawn in the U.S.–Soviet Cold War. The United States and the Soviet Union each gave their support to a different Korean leader. Elections were held in both the south and the north, with the United Nations recognizing only the government from the south, and the Soviet-backed Pyongyang in the north claiming to be the only government on the peninsula. War broke out. An estimated 2.8 million Koreans were killed.

In this climate, my mother became a woman. Because she was the youngest of her family—the same age as her nieces and nephews—she was raised by her brothers from the age of nine, when her mother died from a heart attack. Three months after marrying into a poor family, she was pregnant, widowed by the war, and starving. She came to her rich brothers for help, but they turned her away, saying she belonged to her husband's family because she was a woman. And because she was a woman, she served her mother-in-law for ten years, as a good daughter-in-law should, before her mother-in-law told her to leave her only son and travel to Seoul to find a new husband.

Because my father was the first son in five generations, he had nothing to tie him to North Korea during the war years, so he traveled to the south to begin his life again.

Because his first wife—his two daughters' mother—had abandoned them, my mother dedicated her life to raising the girls as her own, in what mean lifestyle she could provide, her own wealthy upbringing a dim memory.

Sun-Yung, Sun-Mi, Eun-Mi, Mi-Ja, Kyong-Ah! Too many daughters! No sons for Father! What to do? Father says give the youngest two away.

Almost every Korean family has such a story. The characters are always the same: starvation, lost family members, bitter cold, poverty, men unable to support their families, drunkenness, disappointment, despair.

MY SISTERS DO NOT LIKE TO TALK ABOUT the sad stories of the past, so there are still things I do not know. Are we descended from a famous poet or scholar? A philosopher or historian? How far into history can we trace our lineage? Were our grandparents kind?

We don't talk about the people who lived and breathed Confucian morals, whose patriarchal traditions instructed them to abandon our mother when she was hungry and pregnant. What do we care for our impeccable bloodline passed by idle men? Why should we care about our proximity to Korea's fallen nobility, when our queen was stabbed to death more than one hundred years ago and modern Korea—with military conscription and ice cream for all—is a democracy? What does the world care about one woman with three lost children? Who remembers one dead soldier? What does an American care about Japanese aggression before Pearl Harbor? Even the Rape of Nanking hardly registers in the popular consciousness.

But I'm here, one small piece of a great family that somehow survived, albeit in fragments. It is unlikely that my own American children—when they are born and grow into teenagers—will care about a country so far away, about ancestors whose names they cannot pronounce. Their connection to Korea will be even more tenuous than mine, and when I am an old *halmoni* myself, the story of my family will be lost among the stories of all the others whose lives could not be put back into place.

叁

The Happy Village

Once upon a time there was a small village hidden in the mountains. In that village, there lived the happiest people in all of Korea. A laughing river ran through the middle of the village, bringing clean water for all the people. The people loved the river, which provided them with water to drink, to cook, to grow rice, and to wash their white hanboks. The river's laughter echoed throughout the village, spreading joy to all the people.

The happy village was protected by a group of frightening wooden statues at its gate. When the villagers passed the gate, they always placed a small pebble in front of the statues or tied a bright ribbon to the rope fence around them. This brought the village good luck and blessings from the spirit world.

The fame of the happy village swept through every province of Korea, from the Yellow Sea east to the Sea of Korea and north to China. When pilgrims arrived from far away to discover the secret of the happy village, each was made welcome inside the walls and was given a warm place on the floor to sit, plenty of sticky rice, and fresh water from the river.

One night, a dragon came to the village gate. He stopped next to the wooden statues and said to the tallest one, "I have come from far away. I have been very sad, because people fear me. I wish to live in the happy village, where everyone is full of love and happiness."

The tall statue shouted, "You cannot live here! It is my job to keep dragons and evil things like you *out!* That is why the people are happy here."

A silver tear dropped from the dragon's eye. "But I am not evil," he said. "I am just different. If you will let me stay in the village just one night, you will see how good I really am."

The statue looked at him suspiciously, but because he had never seen a dragon cry before, he felt pity for him.

"All right, I suppose you can stay here," said the statue. "But you can't go in. You have to sleep outside the gates."

"Thank you, thank you!" exclaimed the dragon, and he went off into the bamboo a few meters away and fell asleep curled up like a jade ring.

The next night, the dragon again approached the tall statue.

"Please let me inside the gate," he said. "I have shown you that I am a good dragon. I have nowhere else to go."

"You have shown that you can act like a good dragon for one night. That is all. I don't believe that you are a truly good dragon," said the tall statue.

"But I am!" The dragon's silver tears started to flow again.

"Oh, all right," said the tall statue. "I suppose you can stay another night."

"Oh, thank you, thank you!" exclaimed the dragon.

And so the dragon stayed next to the tall statue, hiding in the bamboo, for thirty nights, showing how good he was. He began to get very hungry and thin.

On the thirty-first night, he came to the tall statue again.

"Please," he said, "I'm afraid that I cannot wait much longer. Please let me in."

"You have shown that you can be a good dragon for thirty nights. What if you're a bad dragon on this night? I cannot let you in."

The dragon's eyes filled with silver tears, which fell in twinkling puddles around his feet. "I will never be able to go through the gates," he said to himself. And with that, he shook the silver tears from his feet and walked slowly away from the happy village.

He set his eyes on the North Star and journeyed north toward his homeland, dragging his tail on the cold stone road. He walked many days and many nights, for his sorrow would not permit his tired legs to rest. Finally, he was overcome with thirst, so he made his way beyond the rice paddies, through the hollow reeds, past the long river grass, and down to the riverbank, where he balanced on the slippery, round rocks. But when he dipped his nose into the water, his legs were overcome with weakness, and he slipped into the river. The river pulled him down, down, past dragonflies and lilies, carp and eel, filling his ears and mouth, stealing his breath. Then the light disappeared from his eyes, and he was drowned.

The laughing river closed her arms around the dragon and tasted his kinship with sorrow, warm and sweet, like a ripe peach. She knew in her heart that the dragon was not bad. She sang a smooth lullaby in her liquid voice as she gently rocked the dragon's tired body through the night.

The next morning, the women of the happy village brought their yokes and buckets to the river to carry water home. But no one could explain why, just on that one morning, the laughing river was still, and filled with drops of silver.

Dad stands in the dining room, staring out the window. I crouch in the hallway, unseen.

Outside, it is a clear May morning. The lake is blue and still; the spring turnover has yet to take place. Underneath the dock, a sunfish builds her nest, swishing her tail back and forth in the sand; on the opposite shore, the horses rest their muzzles in the slope of each other's necks. A boy's baseball cap bobs up and down as he pedals his bicycle on the shoulder of Highway 10, where a family passes him on their way to a picnic, coolers full of pop and hot dogs. At the meat market, one of the Johnson boys slices ribs off a beef hung from a hook, while his brother weighs sausage links on butcher paper.

Fifty miles west, Grandma's body descends to the hospital morgue. The sheet slips a little, revealing the same hand that days earlier had been extended to my dad. "Don't tell, Sonny," she had said and squeezed his hand. He nodded. She raised her eyes to the tiled ceiling. "Please, Jesus, take me."

The plains begin at the western edge of Minnesota, where lake country ends. The hayfields are like deserts in their vastness, the way they ripple when the summer wind whistles down from western Canada and through the Red River Valley. Between miles and miles of hayfields, small towns crop up, each one the same with its lone gas station and municipal liquor store.

The eternal hayfields gradually become sugar beet fields, and the odor of sugar processing welcomes travelers to Fargo. For a girl who lived on the outskirts of a small town, Fargo was something of a miracle. It had a shopping mall, bridges, traffic, a hospital with automatic doors.

After her quadruple-bypass surgery, we visited Grandma often. At first, we spent most of our time waiting. We waited to visit her for five minutes every hour while she was in intensive care. When she was moved into a regular room, she showed us the railroad tracks that held her chest together and the place in her leg where they took the artery that now lived in her heart. She seemed to be getting better, despite having been taken completely apart and stapled back together. She made jokes, ate what was on her lunch tray, walked arm-in-arm with my dad down the hallway, put up with his teasing about the back of her gown hanging wide open.

Then she caught a cold. The medication she had been prescribed had destroyed her white blood cells, and without them she was unable to fight the infection. A tube appeared in her nose, sucking out brown fluid that accumulated in a container on the wall. Bruises grew on her arms where the veins refused to cooperate. The hot smell of sickness filled the room. She tired easily. She spoke as if she were dreaming.

Dad's six-foot frame is outlined crisply in the light of the window. He wears Wranglers and Red Wing boots, a leather belt, and no wedding ring—the clothes of a factory worker.

A few minutes earlier, the phone had rung. Mom answered. She took notes in her tight script with a blue ball-point. Grandma had died at five o'clock that morning. She gasped for air a few times, and then it was over.

The plaid on Dad's shirt begins to undulate, like an illusion, a mirage. Then the plaid begins to shake, and his voice chokes, "Why? Why? Why?" The glasses come off, and the rough, workman's hands cover the wet face. The plaid continues to vibrate.

Mom's lips flatten into a tight line, and she walks away from her husband, her shoes *click-click-clicking* neatly on the linoleum, into the kitchen. She runs hot water for dishes, uses extra soap. She opens and closes cupboards quickly, Crisco and flour and sugar *ka-chunking* onto the counter, measuring cups and spatulas busily rattling.

I am glued to my hiding spot. The sticky smell of chocolate brownies fills the house. Dad's shadow pivots around him, grows longer. The plaid shakes.

"You are an emotional girl," my piano teacher remarked.

With notes flying out of the piano, sometimes glittering like fierce icicles, other times embracing each other, each harmony joining hands with the next, I could say anything I wanted. I could conjure up an Ocean Etude, the Winter Wind, the sharp angles of Bartok dwelling in his own Mikrokosmos, the utter longing of poor Johannes Brahms. I could express all the things I felt but was not permitted to say out loud.

It had to be music; other art forms were too dangerous. Poetry and writing can be held in the hands, letters strung together to make words—words that name things for what they are. Painting, too, is dangerous; images and colors—direct, visible—can offend and must be washed away or crumpled and thrown into the garbage.

But music—music is always lovely, especially piano music. No one will guess your thoughts unless they are truly listening.

My piano teacher was listening. "You are an emotional girl," she repeated, as if I didn't know and needed to be told.

She was right on both counts: I was emotional, and I did need to be told.

My mom's perfect, sterilized house almost succeeded in sanitizing the emotion out of me. Lysol, Clorox, ammonia: Let's clean our kitchen and bathroom so they are germ-free, don't forget to dust every day and use Pledge on weekends, don't forget to move the chairs and vacuum underneath, don't forget to use the canister vacuum on the ceiling before guests come over, make sure the towels are always folded in half and then thirds, stack the dishes like this, cut an onion like that, don't leave any skin on the potatoes, weed the garden don't hoe.

After I had moved from the house and had gone through one year of college surrounded by artists whose job it was to emote and had seen a therapist whose job it was to help me figure out what to do with emotions, I would try to draw my mom out, to show her what the feeling world was like.

"Mom, how do you feel about that?"

"What *should* I think about that?"

"It doesn't matter what you think about it. How do you *feel* about it?"

"Don't get smart with me."

The day of Grandma's funeral, the small Methodist church is packed, all the mourners sitting behind the first two pews, which contain our family and that of Dad's sister. Down the row, I can hear my cousins sobbing audibly throughout the last hymn, but I know it is not appropriate to cry. So I hold my breath and add numbers in my head, a strategy that also works at the burial site, when each of my five cousins places a single flower on the coffin, touching its side for the last time. When the last time is not enough, the girls throw themselves onto the coffin again, wailing without shame, and my adult cousins, young men, hang onto each other to keep from collapsing as the body is lowered into the ground.

Dad steals a sideways glance at his sister, whose normally thin face is puffy, and his chin gives him away. "Control yourself," Mom preempts him.

I want to go back into the memory the day his mother died. "Here. Here's a Kleenex for you. I'm so sorry. I'm sad, too." I want to pat the cushion next to me—"Let's sit down together"—coax the feelings out, sit with him and take his hands in mine, rub the back of his smooth cotton work shirt.

But I did not say those things and I did not do those things, because at twelve years old I still did not know how and because the right thing to do—as demonstrated by my mom—was to pretend that bad things don't happen, to be strong and silent for my dad.

And so from my hiding spot I watched the plaid shake, listened to my mom rattle dirty bowls in the sink, and felt the loneliness grow.

The fat auctioneer in the white cowboy hat and his plaid-shirted assistant run the best show in town. The auctioneer, a living testament to what too many corndogs can do to your waist, waves his wooden cane in the air and chants his hypnotic poem while the plaid shirt man points and yells at bidders, who solemnly raise their bidding number on manila cards. The rest of the crowd is stone still and pokerfaced, so as not to be mistaken for someone bidding.

— Five dolla five dolla five and five and five five
    do I hear five—
        — Yyyy-ep!
— Six and six do I hear six gimmee six—
        — Yyyy-ep!
— She says six and six do I hear seven seven seven
    anybody seven do I hear seven going once and twice
    and SOoooLD! To num-ber twenty.
Men in feed-n-seed hats, each with his own missus in an appliqué sweatshirt, bid on the remnants of bankrupt farms, the stuff that

nobody else wanted when grandma died, the material things that can't fit inside the shared bedroom of a nursing home. They line up to claim the spoils, vinyl wallets in one hand, greasy white envelopes of mini-donuts in the other.

The auction pros set up here last night, rolling in the snack wagon and the portable blue biffy, bringing out items piled all catawampus. They lined the perimeter of the hay wagon with the boxes and opened up this morning at seven so the bidders could dig through the stuff and decide on their purchase goals.

The plaid shirt man brings the next cardboard box to the auctioneer, who wipes underneath his aviators with a white hanky.

— Ladies and gentlemen, we have here a box of miscellaneous kitchenware and home décor items. There is a gen-you-wine oil painting here on the top and right here we've got a fine set of Tupperware, all you could want ladies, we've got the Jell-O molds and the pickle container and more sandwich boxes than you can shake a stick at. There's much too much in here for me to tell you all about right now. Earl, let's sell the whole box. The whole shebang, ladies.

Mom glances at her list. Yes, this one's on it. She wants it for the sandwich boxes, and she's made a note to herself that she'll go up to five dollars for the whole box. She fingers her manila bidding number in anticipation.

— Someone start the bidding someone start the bidding let's go let's go how bout two gimmee two—
    Mom's hand shoots up.
    — Yyy-ep!
— Okay now here we go gimmee three and three do I hear three—

Another woman's hand pops up not far away. Mom immediately recognizes her: Betty, that divorced alcoholic. She's the person who tries to outbid everyone just out of spite. Mom decides that she will not lose to her this time.

— Yyy-ep!
— Four and a four gimme four let's go do I hear four—
    Mom nods.
        — Yyy-ep!
— Five do I hear five—
            Betty nods.
        — Yyy-ep!
— Six and a six do I hear six—
    Mom.
        — Yyy-ep!
— Seven gimme seven gotta gimme seven seven seven
    let's go seven—
            Betty.
        — Yyy-ep!
— She says seven gimme eight how's eight and eight
    do I hear eight—
Mom glances at her list. The limit she set was five dollars. She can feel that Tupperware slipping away from her, can't bear the thought of Betty one-upping her yet again. She nods, resolute, and raises her hand.
        — Yyy-ep!
— Alright nine gimme nine and nine and gimme nine
    and nine do I hear nine—
Betty raises her number, obnoxious as ever, and you can bet just ready to bid as high as she wants to even though she's probably on disability.
        — Yyy-ep!
— Do I hear—
Desperate, Mom calls upon her most intimidating auction strategy: she looks the auctioneer right in the aviators and nods quickly several times in a row. Dang her five-dollar limit: she will not lose to that woman again.
    — twelve! and—
        — Yyy-ep!

—Okay how's fourteen fourteen Betty gimme fourteen
do I hear fourteen—
Come on Betty, I dare you.
— let's go fourteen Betty gimme fourteen fourteen
fourteen—
Just try and outbid me again.
— going once going twice and it is SOoold! To Margaret
Brauer for twelve dollars. Congratulations Margaret.

Mom beams triumphantly at the auctioneer and purposely avoids looking at Betty, who is wondering if maybe Margaret will take a couple dollars for that Jell-O mold.

Mom scratches "Tupperware" off her list. She has also purchased a carnival glass candy bowl, a collectible figurine, and fourteen apple-shaped plates today. She didn't get the antique trunk, but who can win with those antique dealers from the Cities coming up here and raising all the prices?

She picks up her box and pays for it in cash, then orders Dad to carry it back to the pickup. He stops at the snack wagon on the way and buys a couple of chocolate-chip cookies and root beers.

The sun is hot inside the pickup, where Carol and I sit alternately reading books, napping, and cross-stitching.

"Thanks, Dad!" we chirp as he hands us each a can of pop and a cookie. "Whadja get?"

"Well, I didn't get nothink but your mother got this here box of junk," he says, as he adds it to the other two boxes in the back of the pickup.

I jump into the back to take a look.

"Find anythink good der, Skeeziks?" Dad smiles his bright smile.

"What's this?" I pull out a shallow box, one side made of glass, the rest made out of wood.

"Lemme see that." Carol pokes her head out of the cab of the truck and holds her hand out. She takes a quick look. "It's a shadow box," she declares flatly.

"It's a what kinda box?" Dad asks.

"A shadow box. I saw one in biology." Carol pushes it back into my hands and continues sipping root beer through a bendy straw and reading *Gone with the Wind*.

"Isn't that somethink?" says Dad, as he looks over the side of the truck where I sit on the hump of the wheel well.

"Some*thing*." Mom has been trying to correct Dad's pronunciation of words ending in "ing" for years, to no avail. I make it part of my household responsibility to be part of the grammar and pronunciation Gestapo.

"Well, ex-cuuuuuuse me," Dad says in the most melismatic way possible, extending "excuse" out into a four-syllable word.

"Sorry," I say, not apologetically at all. Dad walks off in a huff.

The shadow box is homemade, sanded and stained in an amateurish way, the glass the garage-door type you can get cut in the hardware store. The butterflies are pinned in rows with their names pasted below them: Spicebush Swallowtail, Hackberry Emperor, Painted Lady, Monarch.

I like the butterflies so much that I ask my mom for permission to keep the box for myself, and she says, "why, of course yes." We clean it off together, careful not to dislodge the butterflies. We mount a new hook on the back and find a place of honor in my bedroom, on the wall next to the knick-knack shelf, with my collection of miniature wind-up vacuum cleaners, blenders, and sewing machines. Every Saturday, I dust my knick-knacks and butterfly shadow box with Pledge and memorize the patterns on the wings, thinking today I might be lucky enough to catch a butterfly myself and put it in a jar.

Inside the shadow box, the butterflies hang in frozen rows, wings neatly pinned as if suspended in mid-flight. They have forgotten what it was to be a larva and then a chrysalis, have forgotten the struggle of transformation and the panic of asphyxiation inside the killing jar, and now hang displayed, oblivious, a negligible blip of absence in the memory of one wildflower patch on a bankrupt farm.

ASIAN CHILDREN: China dolls, whiz kids, happy,
    cooperative, obedient
ASIAN WOMEN: exotic, petite, lotus blossoms, pale,
    fragile, docile, geishas
ASIAN MEN: yellow, menacing, buck-toothed, greasy,
    suspicious, emasculated

It is easy to see why parents who want only the best for their daughters prefer that they date only real Americans.

I had a couple of boyfriends in high school. Both were Hmong. The first had emigrated from Laos with his family as a project of our church: Lutheran offerings paid their way here and provided a place to stay, and then the whole family took over the post of church janitorial staff.

The eldest son grew up to be the star kicker on the Hornets football team, an adequate basketball player (fast, but not tall enough), and a peripheral of the semi-popular crowd. I liked him. He was kind to me. It seemed natural that he and I would go bowling together and take walks after school, sipping juice boxes we bought at the corner store. I bought him a blue sweater from J.C. Penney. He presented me with a tiny Buddha on a chain, a treasured possession given him by his uncle. I thought I would surely go to hell for having a Buddha in my pocket, so I invited him to my Bible study and set about trying to convert him. I made word puzzles on notebook paper for him to decode; he always figured them out. We never kissed or even held hands, but we were genuinely fond of each other. I put the Buddha in a safe place in my dresser, inside a box, two layers of waterproof packing tape wrapped around it to seal in the sin.

The next boyfriend must have found me beautiful because he saw me once and dropped his immensely popular and white girlfriend and began to date me. He was a young man from Thailand who attended community college about forty miles away. He drove to my house on the weekends to pick me up, then drove us all the way back to his house, where we watched TV and ate whatever his little sister had slavishly cooked that day—sometimes a fish on newspaper, other times noodles or vegetables. His house smelled strange, and inside it was almost bare: a poor immigrant's house overlooking the Dairy Queen.

My boyfriend was almost six feet tall, muscular, model-like. He got his hair to do things in the front. He wore an acid-washed jean jacket, which he later gave to me, shiny leather shoes, white button-down shirts that emphasized the beauty of his toffee-colored skin. He was the deliverer of my first kiss, in the car after a high school cafeteria dance.

I NEVER DATED AN ASIAN MAN AGAIN.

"Who do you think I am?" I screamed at my dad. He mocked their faces, as if they were not human, but dark, stupid monkeys. He mutilated their long names, which he could not and did not want to pronounce correctly.

"His name is— " I spat, five syllables sprayed out in a volley, as if to attack his mouth and the singsong words that came out of it, humiliating my boyfriend behind his back, humiliating me to my face. That butterflies-in-the-stomach feeling I always had before a date wasn't lovesickness: it was self-loathing, the kind you get when you discover that you must be one of two things to your dad, either invisible or ridiculous; the kind you get when you hate your own face, so much like your boyfriend's and so easily mocked; the kind you get when you want to love your father but hate him instead.

It was during those years that I took down the bulletin board in my bedroom and with a thumbtack scratched my Korean name (which I had cunningly memorized years before) into the paint on the wall and then replaced the bulletin board so I would not be found out.

It was also during those years that I permed my hair beyond recognition, into a giant mass of curls. Mom loved it. If my hair was parallel to the floor, all the better. In this respect I was successful. However, my stubborn black hair refused to lighten, no matter how much peroxide or lemon juice I poured on it, no matter how long I sat in the sun. I continued to perm and peroxide until my hair broke off in chunks.

There were all kinds of things that *Teen* magazine, *Glamour, Young Miss,* and *Seventeen* recommended I do to make myself beautiful, but my face wasn't getting any less round, my eyebrows wouldn't stop growing downward, and the curling-the-eyelashes trick usually ended up in a smashed–spider legs look.

Later, my Korean mother would ask me if I dated Korean men. It was not so much a question as a request: her wish, the same as that of all the members of the old generation, was to have one-hundred-percent-Korean grandchildren. "No, Umma," was my answer. "There are no Asian people where I live."

Sometime during my teenaged years I must have forgotten my vow to be perfect.

"You're not my real mom, anyway!"

There. I said it. Or rather, I yelled it. I had resisted yelling it before, knowing that it was rotten to say and I should never say it, and also knowing that it would work best the first time and I had better be good and mad when I used my trump card.

I looked at my mom, daring her to tell me that I wasn't her real daughter, either. She didn't. Her face didn't even change expression. No reaction at all.

I stomped down the hallway and banged my bedroom door shut.

Of course, my "real" mom was never around to say no to me, to tell me I couldn't go skiing with my friends because it was piano lesson day, or that I couldn't go to an Amy Grant concert because it was a *rock* concert (some kind of trouble would certainly be brewing there, and in *Fargo,* too), or that I couldn't do basically whatever I wanted.

No, the dirty work was left up to Margaret.

She was also the person to keep me in the house when I just had to get out, just wanted to go for a walk to *get out of the house* for just an hour, the person who tackled me in the snow out of principle because she wanted me to be *inside* the house, not *outside,* yelling at me, screaming that I would give her a cancerous tumor when I gave her a kick in the leg, and not as hard as I could have, either. She was the person to drag me out from underneath the bed, peeling my fingers from the bed frame, when waking up before dawn to catch the bus didn't suit me.

I went to school only because I had to, went to graduation only because I had to. My cross to bear that day was walking down the aisle with Chad Peterson in front of all of Harlow, while all the others were walking with their sweethearts. I had to walk with the same kid I had to sit by in fifth grade when nobody else would sit by either of us, Chad Peterson, who was about twenty-five at the time of graduation, who smelled like pickles and wore a Ski-Doo hat all winter, indoors and out, and who never stopped doing Fonzie imitations. "Ayyyy," he would say over and over again, extending his thumbs and leaning back, all crooked teeth and wiry beard stubble.

I was reduced to this on graduation day. We probably all felt mortified, with the exception of a few: the blonde-haloed athlete and cheerleader types who were equally paired in beauty and popularity ever since we started wearing deodorant, who ended up marrying their high school sweethearts and never moving away. There was no reason to move: life was good enough right there.

I fantasized about running away. With my sister in college, I figured I could just ride my bike into town and catch a Greyhound bus from Riewer's gas station into the Cities. I could live in my sister's dorm. But I never got as far as making a real plan or even packing. I suppose somewhere there was the memory of my sister packing her bags to run away when she was a child, and my mom didn't cry or protest but instead helped her gather her things. I knew running away wouldn't hurt anyone but myself, and I was a coward, so I stayed, got confirmed, graduated, counted the days until I could leave Harlow and never come back.

The first time I went to Korea, I didn't meet my younger sister for a week because she was busy running away from our Korean mom.

Whether the adoption agency had stopped her, or whether she waited until she thought I was old enough or her own life happy enough to be presented, I don't know. Whatever the reason, my Korean mother's policy of non-interference lasted from the first Christmas I spent in the United States until the winter of my junior year in high school.

It was on one of those brittle white days that I stood at the end of the driveway at the mailbox, the school bus disappearing around the curve. The envelope was thick underneath my mittens, elation hot on my cheeks, the clear blue sky cupping Harlow and Seoul and every place in between underneath its wide arc.

I ran up the driveway, tearing apart the envelope as I went, opened the door with the hidden key, dropped my school bag on the floor, shed my coat and boots, scrutinized the photographs, read the letter, read it again, and called the one person I thought would care: Darren—my alternately pink- and green-haired, music-loving, fashion-conscious friend and neighbor.

I was surprised that the significance of the letter somehow escaped him. I thought he might want to come over to my house and see it for himself—touch the papers reverently, study the faces, compare me to my family. But he didn't seem to understand the importance of what had just happened. This was hardly his fault: since I never spoke of my family aloud the way I thought of them inside, how could anyone realize how important they were to me?

That night, I was granted permission to call the phone number written at the bottom of the letter. I was nervous, wanting to chatter about what to say, what to do if someone besides my mother answered, what to do if no one answered. I finally summoned the courage to dial the longest number I'd ever seen. But no one else made an event out of this momentous occasion. My parents did not gather around me to hear the conversation; instead, they went about their own business—watching TV, organizing grocery lists.

My memory of the night I heard my mother's voice is recorded from the vantage point of one who has left the body. It is as if I were pinned to the ceiling of the world, looking down upon myself through the roof of our house. I am in a dark room in a dark corner, but I am radiant. There is nothing in my sight but me, a dim lamp, and a miraculous telephone connecting me to the other side of the world, to my mother, who could say nothing but my name, over and over in her breaking voice, "Kyong-Ah. Kyong-Ah."

It is not supposed to happen this way, and I have never heard another story in which a Korean birth mother finds her child and not the other way around. Who but Umma could have done it—with no money to bribe, no helpful husband, no English skills, and hardly an education? She had only her determination, and enough of it for an army of men.

When we finally met six years after that letter arrived, Umma told me that she had gotten my address by going to the agency and waiting until Mrs. Chong would give it to her. How long do you have to wait to be given something you're under no circumstances supposed to have? There are rules and regulations for this sort of thing, and they involve "non-identifying" information that is doled out through the middleman of the adoption or social welfare agency. Yet she was somehow able to get *very* identifying information: my parents' names, their address, their ages, a photograph—all the information the agency had collected. Umma must have set up camp in that office and stayed there for days, eating her meals out of plastic bags and nodding off on a bench. They probably yelled at her and dragged her out time and again, until finally Mrs. Chong was so sick of her that she handed over the information just to get rid of the nuisance. Then it was Umma's sheer force of will that kept us tenuously together throughout the years and—if this really was the first letter she sent after the gift of hanboks that first Christmas—a show of incredible restraint on her part that she waited seventeen years to use the information.

IN THE SIX YEARS SEPARATING THE FIRST LETTER and our reunion, we exchanged letters that my American mother did not hide from me; she even forwarded them to me when I was away at college. My mother's letters were beautiful chunks of nothingness describing mountains, weather, the blossoms on trees—a particularly Korean (or Minnesotan?) affectation. Perhaps it was a necessary affectation if any communication was to happen at all; the phrasebooks my sisters carefully copied from were not designed to answer probing questions from long-lost overseas daughters.

"The best season for reading," my sister wrote. "Fine weather a clear sky and fresh air sometimes makes me happy. Autumn is really here. A single leaf falling is a sign of fall coming. Seoul of the present time is very beautiful. Fall is my favorite season."

We spent three years writing about picnics, vacations, Korean traditions. Three years of sentiments and exchanges of pictures, but no mention of why I was here and they were there.

Being selfish and frustrated, I finally forced the relationship my way, saying, "I am asking for the last time why you gave us away. Why? If you do not answer me, I will no longer write to you."

The answer was swift and long. It began "Dear my daughters Mi-Ja, Kyong-Ah!

> I wish Father, Mother in U.S.A. are in good health and enjoy increasing prosperity in the present business in 1992.
>
> One year had passed and the 20 years already passed after sending you to the United States is unfamiliar. I was in pain due to your difficult conditions.
>
> Let me try to recall my home's sad story. It was not a happy home even before our separation. . . .

The letters—both the polite, chatty ones and the emotional ones that could only be written with the aid of someone who possessed the kind of education or experience that Umma could never buy—instigated a kind of alchemical reaction. The thin *par avion* envelopes, the accented English written perfectly and without a slant, the stamps with strange pictures of birds and tortoises, celadon, and important Korean people and landmarks—these all conspired to reorder my world beginning with a simple pastime: the subversive act of noticing things.

Because when my body is falling it moves faster than when I move it myself; because the state of the exile is suspension, caught in the middle of an arc, between psyche, body, and place (neither, nor, both, between); because the essence of that which is most present is not visible (like love, like your own eye, like an elusive element leaving only its shadow [evidence of its supposed existence] in a closed laboratory); because life is a ballet of consecutive moments—the grace is in the margins.

When I first moved to the Twin Cities, my white Wisconsinite roommate and I had a favorite game that we played each time we went to Target. (Target is the great unifier in Minnesota—everyone, regardless of class, age, or race, ends up there to buy toilet paper, toothpaste, household items, and automotive supplies.) The game—useful for two roommates from small midwestern towns and evolving over several trips—was called "Name that Asian." I had seen Asian people only at piano contests held in Moorhead; to have repeated access to Asian-gawking was fun and educational.

We developed guidelines for distinguishing between Asians as we sat next to the door, watching people file in and grab their carts. The guidelines for women, loosely, were:

1. CHINESE: Rounder and paler.
2. HMONG: Smaller and darker. Wears very yellow gold jewelry with filigree, usually steps out of a flashy sports car, travels in large groups of other Hmong.
3. JAPANESE: Something about the nose, and for younger women, that excruciatingly cute processed hair and pastel clothes thing.
4. KOREAN KOREAN: Brownish hair, speaks English with an accent, fake designer shoes and handbag, matching husband and kids.
5. ADOPTED KOREAN: Brownish hair, speaks English with no accent, sweatshirt and jeans, goes shopping with and dates white people.

Asians were scary. Other. Something to be examined. We had no way of knowing if our hideous generalizations were the least bit accurate, but we were—or at least I was—curious about who was who and how I fit into the scheme of things.

Suddenly there were Asians and lots of them, but I had my reasons for not attending any Pan-Asian student events during college. For instance, I couldn't think of anything more uncomfortable than going to a Lunar New Year party. When the hell is Lunar New Year, anyway, and how did they come up with that calendar, and what year is it? My knowledge of the Chinese zodiac was gleaned from paper place mats in restaurants. I walked by the party in the basement of the student union, head down, pretending to be on my way somewhere else, leaving my options open. I shot a quick sideways glance into the rec center. The place was filled with Asians. Asian Asians. Ugh. I didn't know anyone. What was I supposed to do if I went in there? Introduce myself as Jane the Twinkie, the Pan-Asian fraud? Stand around with an egg roll in my hand and wait for someone to talk to me in English so accented I couldn't understand it or, worse yet, talk to me in Korean? Excruciating. I kept walking.

Yet it was the presence of organizations like the Pan-Asian student group that fostered the kind of tolerance on campus that surprised— no, that's not a strong enough word—*boggled* me. All year, I kept waiting for the inevitable slurs, whether in private or in front of a teacher. I braced myself for them. I retained my tough skin. At first, I counted the absence of racial epithets by months. First one month, then two. Then three. Then I counted by semesters. At the end of my freshman year, I realized with no small amount of amazement that I had attended school for an entire year without hearing the word "chink." I felt my self-confidence grow; I had more friends than ever; I was almost beautiful. I nearly forgot that I was a chink until the night before I was to return to Harlow.

肆

SWM, 29, SEEKS ASIAN
You: Submissive, petite, long hair.
Your master is 6'3", brown/brown,
185 lbs. Looking for fun. Will
respond to all that send pictures.
Mailbox #14520.

> When your father got free, he looking for a chance to
> find us under the ground of Residence Register Card
> and we had to went on moving here and there to refuge
> from your father.

Sometimes I think there must be an astrological perfection to the order of the world, a plan put forth by a force that transcends political, cultural, and temporal boundaries, a force so great that it encompasses both Buddhist hearts and Lutheran ones, as well as the ones who have lost faith in anything.

My mother's life wrapped itself around mine in an echo, the way a small pebble thrown into the water makes larger and larger ripples around itself. In this reverberation, I experienced the fear that my mother had given me away to escape.

This fear has a set of symptoms that I know well: insomnia, shortness of breath, frustration and boredom borne out of the inability to focus on a task. It is two black half-moons underneath my eyes, a chill accompanied by shaking, the cold glass of water I gulp after such an episode.

"Mr. Jeong" was what I called my mental illness for years, thinking that it was my father's fault—his addictive, murderous genes brewing in me. I still believe my elders have imparted things to me, but not through the body alone: the pulse of emotion, carried by an invisible artery, ties me to events, to lives, to repeated cycles—no matter what side of the world I call home.

On frequent mornings, during the three or four seconds between waking and emerging from the residue of a dream, there is a moment of disorientation that collapses time and swirls the years together so that my present is indistinguishable from my past. These moments are a touchstone, a reminder that although time seems to pass in orderly, pie-shaped increments, I am wherever—and whenever—my memory drops me.

I call him "my stalker." I know his full name, his Minnesota court file number, his U.S. Department of Justice register number. But I define him by his purpose, his activity in my life, just as I refer to others as "my doctor," "my teacher," or "my hairdresser." He is my stalker. He stalks me.

It doesn't matter that he's been in jail for almost twelve years. It doesn't matter that I've spoken to him only three times. His presence in my consciousness has little to do with physical proximity: he floats around inside my brain. Sometimes he is overwhelming; sometimes he is hardly noticeable, but, like white noise, he never stops.

He's there when I go out in public, humming around in the back of my thoughts, a reminder to stay alert, walk tall, hold my keys so they are ready to be used either to unlock my car or to defend myself. He was there when I shaved my black hair completely to the scalp, washed off my make-up, and donned used men's clothes and a baseball cap in an effort to conceal my femininity. He's there when I hear loud sounds in the duplex downstairs and I have to restrain myself from calling my husband at work, begging him to come home. He was there this morning when I woke from a nightmare, heart racing and filled with anger because this squatter in my life refuses to leave.

Jung, schmung: it doesn't take a depth psychologist to figure out what my dreams are about. Here's the dream from this morning: I'm completely naked, and I know I'm being chased. There's a man in a car who tells me that, in the plan to shake off the stalker, I'm the decoy, and I'm supposed to walk in the street in one direction to get the stalker to follow me, and at the last moment my helper man will zoom by in the other direction and pick me up, leaving the stalker driving in the wrong direction, and we'll get away. That's the plan, but at the last moment my helper man disappears and I'm left alone, running naked from my stalker with my bare feet on a street covered in broken glass. I search frantically for a weapon, but I can't find anything, and then I wake up.

For a long time, I dreamt that I was a rabbit. I was sitting right at the hunter's feet; I knew I had to remain perfectly still or I would be seen. So I waited for the hunter to move on—not daring to even blink or breathe—but he didn't.

My other recurrent dream is more mundane but also more realistic. There's someone breaking into my house. He is at the back door close to where I sleep. I can hear him—I know he's there—but my fear paralyzes me and I can't do anything about it.

These days, I don't watch anything that portrays stalking. Even though people recommend this interesting TV program or that good movie, I don't mind limiting my choices in drama, action/suspense, news reporting, and even comedy: stalker stories are not entertainment for me.

How about this: I'll tell you a real story about a young co-ed who was almost raped and murdered by a deranged stalker. There are guns and videotapes in this story, police and courts. As the story continues, the young co-ed goes crazy and ends up in the nut bin, drugged and surrounded by people falling asleep on their lunch trays because they've just had shock treatment. Here's the story, and I won't even charge you admission.

I WAS A FRESHMAN AT AUGSBURG COLLEGE in Minneapolis, awarded a full-tuition academic scholarship, double majoring, awards coming out of my ears. I actually had to turn down scholarship money because they don't allow you to make a profit. Smart in school—dumb in life.

It began with a phone call.

"I've seen you around on campus," he said. "Would you like to go out with me?"

Even though I knew that the Augsburg photo directory was the primary date procurement aid on campus—how else would he have gotten my number?—there was something about the unexpectedness of the call that made me wonder.

Being polite, I said, "Well, I already have a boyfriend, but I'm going to band right now, so if you want to meet me in the lobby, I'll walk across the street with you."

He met me, we walked through the skyway and across the street, and that was it.

Until the messages came.

I took the tapes—full of long, distorted love songs—out of my answering machine and brought them to the head of campus security. I told her I was getting creepy messages, some strange songs on my answering machine, threatening calls mentioning my boyfriend. I had a gut feeling about who was making the calls. She took the tapes and promptly lost them.

Next, a trick. As my boyfriend and I found that we had not much more in common than sheer geekiness—*What do you want to do? I don't know. What do you want to do?*—I started entertaining the idea of seeing other people.

My date was tall, handsome, a hockey player. He checked out well with the other girls in the dorm. They knew him, he was a good guy, they said. I had met him a couple of times as he visited the girls next door. They were popular, the kind of girls who aren't afraid to go to parties in frat house basements, who don't religiously iron their blouses on Friday nights after they finish their homework. I could see they were surprised that he asked me out, but he came to pick me up on time, and we went for a walk across Riverside Avenue, into the U of M campus, past Wilson Library, and onto the Washington Bridge.

On my second and last date with him, he asked me to come up to his dorm—the building connected by a small lobby to mine. He greeted me at the door, then excused himself to brush his teeth. I stood in the kitchen, waiting nervously.

The stalker turned out to be his roommate and best friend.

He materialized, as he was wont to do over the next few months, a complete surprise to me. They call it the "freeze response"—what some people do in times of danger. Here's what it feels like: everything is very vivid, and you are very alive, but there's an element of the surreal about it, and you're trying to get yourself together and think, but you know lots of things are just sliding right past you. I think this is what a rabbit feels like right before a hawk's talons sink into its soft neck.

"You're nothing but a Korean in a white man's society. You're a gook, you're a chink."

I don't remember the other things he said, but I know the words came out and came out some more. I remember slapping him as hard as I could, open-handed, and how very solid he was. He didn't move at all; he wasn't affected; he just smiled at me. I pushed my way past him and ran down the stairs, not wanting to wait for the elevator to trundle its way up to floor thirteen, stopped halfway down and cried underneath the big number eight.

A videotape of this incident was collected later as evidence. I never saw it; I'm not sure if it was because I was being "protected" or if it was because in a criminal case the plaintiff is the State, not the victim. I never saw the other videotapes that he had filmed of me, either—videos of me brushing my hair, getting ready for school, everyday things in front of the window, captured because I loved the sunshine and the fresh air and because he lived on the thirteenth floor and I lived on the seventh floor of the adjacent building.

It was close to the end of the school year, and I was planning on spending the summer at home, anyway. I missed Mom and Dad, trees and water. I had already finished taking my finals. I called my parents, and, although I didn't ask them to, they immediately jumped into their Ford pickup truck and drove four hours to retrieve me. I called security at the school and they made a report.

When I think about it now, I'm not sure what tipped me off that something was very, very wrong. It could have easily been a date gone bad. But there was something so twisted about it, the whole setup, that I think I knew in my gut that I was in danger.

Summer started out plainly enough: I was a check-out girl at the supermarket in the next town west, which was big enough to have its own McDonald's. I schemed for something better, and my hustling soon paid off: I was hired as a pianist at a couple of local restaurants, and between two happy hours I managed to earn a respectable sum without having to endure the drudgery of memorizing a hundred produce codes. I turned in my blue checker's smock and said good-bye to all those food stamps and coupons.

It was August, the hottest weeks of the year in Minnesota, when I parked my '76 Malibu Classic in the back lot of Jerry B's for afternoon happy hour. He materialized in my open car window.

"I just want to say I'm sorry for last spring," he said.

Stuffed into the window, his body blocked out the light. I could feel his breath close to my face.

"Well, you better be," was the first and only thing I could think to say as I launched myself out of the car. Fear has its own, immediate logic: I didn't try to figure out why he was there by saying, "Well, hey, what are you doing up in these parts?" I didn't scan the parking lot to see what kind of car he drove. There was no weighing of options; I just ran into the restaurant as fast as I could.

So many parts are missing. I know I called my dad then; I remember dialing furiously, panicked. I remember the square, silver buttons of the pay phone. I don't remember if I came home or stayed at work, or what my dad said. Maybe I don't remember so that I can bear it.

The next part I remember is driving up to our tuck-under garage on a Sunday night after our family vacation in Wisconsin. I've always slept in the car, tending to become carsick if awake. It was late at night, completely dark, my dad at the wheel, my mom in the passenger's seat, me horizontal in the back seat.

"Someone's broken into the house!" Mom's voice was shrill, taut. The headlights shone on the broken glass of the garage door window. We called the sheriff—was it from the neighbor's house? Was it from our own house? How did we know it was safe to go in? So much is missing from my memory.

What I do remember is humiliation.

The humiliation of having to use the toilet after this long ride home from vacation and not being able to because our house had been wrecked and we couldn't touch anything; our bathroom was covered in dirt, used by my stalker. So I had to squat in the woods next to our house; in the dark night, I soiled my own clothing.

Humiliation when the two men from the sheriff's department finally showed up, forty-five minutes later, and I said *I know who did this,* and they didn't believe me, wouldn't even talk to me like an adult.

"I know who did this."

"Was it your boyfriend?"

"No it's not my boyfriend. It's this guy from my college, but I don't even know him."

"Sounds like it's her boyfriend."

IT WAS IN THOSE DAYS THAT I STARTED TO SLEEP flat on my back, glasses perched watchfully over my closed eyes. But my glasses didn't help me see in the dark.

I awoke in the middle of the night to a rhythmic, creaking sound. *Creak-rip, creak-rip, creak-rip.* In my sleepy state, I thought it must be my parents having sex. *That's a new one,* I thought. *Never heard that before.* My room was at the opposite end of the hallway from my parents', close enough to hear them snoring at night, close enough to hear anything at all. Rational deduction set in a few seconds later: My parents don't have sex.

"Mom, I hear something!" I hissed down the hall, terrified, stuck to my bed with my silly glasses in the dark, not daring to move.

"I hear it, too!" her steely, tight voice answered back.

The man of the house was sleeping soundly. Old-fashioned females, we expected him to take care of things.

Dad, wake up.

He finally woke and turned on the lights inside the house. It was over as soon as the house was brightly illuminated from the inside; Dad said he saw the stalker running down the hill of our lawn.

HOME REPAIR WAS NEEDED. In the first break-in, things got dirty. Mom cleaned. I straightened up my bedroom. The lawn was torn up by a car that had been driven over the retaining wall. A basement window was broken and the garage door window, too. Now a screen had to be fixed; the stalker had tried to cut it away while we were sleeping.

He's a stalker. He knows when you're there and when you're not. He was getting brave, breaking in while we were home, wanting what? At the time we could only guess. Later, I found out exactly what he wanted. The psychological evaluation of 1991 made the following statement:

> This individual had a .38 caliber pistol in his possession
> during the commission of this crime with the basic intentions
> of kidnapping Jane, raping her, and then killing her. In fact,
> the Defendant was candid enough to admit that he purchased
> video camera equipment so that he could record his exploits
> of raping and killing the intended victim so that he could
> further enjoy the experience again and again later on . . .

By this time, we had alerted our next-door neighbors to the strange circumstances of our summer.

The phone rang at four o'clock in the morning. There was a car driving back and forth slowly in front of our houses, Ross said. Dad was out the door in a minute, running across the lawn into the neighbor's garage, hopping into the car with Ross and rolling down to the end of the driveway. Dad had one mission: get the license plate number.

Armed with a pen and a notepad, Dad and Ross sat at the bottom of the driveway, waiting for the car to pass again. Meanwhile, Mom was on the phone with 9-1-1. She was repeating herself over and over; I could hear the frustration rising in her voice as she tried to convince the operator that this was serious business. Outside, it was pitch black; rural roads don't have lights. I stood a few feet away from my mom, completely impotent, frozen, blind.

Then there were shots.

How many? Later, nobody could agree on the number. Three? Six? Who thinks to stand there and count?

What I do remember so clearly is the sound of the shots, the way they popped like giant, hateful balloons, the way the silences in between, packed with uncertainty—is my dad alive or dead?—were fathomless, terrifying.

Then Mom was *screaming* into the phone, "There's shots! There's shots!" I stood completely silent, frozen again, useless.

Interrogation, August 12, 1991:

> Q. You could a killed him you mean . . .
> A. Well, I mean if I was the kind of person I could of, but all I wanted to do was I was annoyed at him and I was in a bad mood and wanted to scare him. So I just put three bullets in the . . . right headlight.
> Q. He was standing there—they were in the car when you did this?
> A. The guy was—he was—yeah, he was in his car.
> Q. Ah-huh. You weren't afraid you were gonna hit him?
> A. Oh, I was like point blank range, I mean if I wanted to hit him I could a hit him. I mean I'm not that bad of a shot . . .

The sounds of the shots would come back to me later: in class, in the grocery store, at night. The slightest loud noise made me jump and yelp. Balloons popping—terrible. Loud motorcycles— another anxiety attack. Forget Fourth of July fireworks.

I've imagined the scenario thousands of times since then. *What if. What if I wasn't frozen? What if I see him again? What will I do?*

There was a time when I wouldn't have chosen my life over his. I emerged from college four years later beaten up emotionally, intermittently suicidal, with no further plans because I didn't think I would live that long. I hated myself—for what I had brought on my family, for being worthless, for being someone whom no one would take seriously. My Lutheran God hadn't answered my prayers, so I began to attend a "spiritually diverse community church" where I learned that sometimes our souls make pacts with other souls while they're floating around out there in the ether, before being reincarnated yet again. "That's how you learn your life lessons," the spiritual leader said. "You made an agreement with your stalker for him to do this to you, so you could learn." Translation: I wanted it. *It was my fault.*

The sheriff's department came out about forty-five minutes after the shooting. I'm glad that no one was actually shot; they would have been dead by the time an ambulance arrived.

Somehow, we finally got real help from the Lakes Crisis Center, a women's group specializing in domestic and sexual abuse. "Rattle their cages," is what Cyndi called it. "I'm going to go down to the courthouse and rattle their cages."

Things started happening thanks to Cyndi, who, believe me, sees more shit on a daily basis than you can ever imagine in your entire life. I spent some days hanging around in her office, a "safe place," watching the women go in and out. Women with barefoot kids who were obviously abused by their husbands, women who looked like they were straight out of a *National Geographic* article about places in Appalachia so isolated that the people still speak Elizabethan English. Cyndi gave out clothes, food, toys, advice.

She knew how to throw around her blessed two hundred pounds

to produce some action. She knew how to get past the dithering secretaries, how to talk to men so they would listen. I liked her.

Cyndi showed us how to obtain a restraining order. She was realistic about it; she said that a restraining order doesn't do any good if the person has decided he's not going to follow laws, but since my stalker already knew where we lived—the restraining order discloses the address—we might as well get one. At least when he was arrested it would be one more violation on his record.

Suddenly, there was an empty sheriff's car parked in front of our house as a deterrent, and we moved out of our house. Our new residence was a cabin out of view of the road, equipped with a small kitchen and beds, a TV. I was instructed to stay at the cabin and not go near the road or anywhere I would be seen.

Mom and Dad were allowed to go only to work, nowhere else, so Cyndi brought us packaged deli food—pre-made Jell-O in plastic molds, sandwich fixings, chips—and we waited. I slept, chewed my nails, wrote letters to my friends, tore birch bark off trees.

It's been said that the way to make caged rats crazy is to shock them at random. Take away all of their control, take away any kind of reason behind the electric stimulus—no association to the little bar that dispenses food pellets—and they'll die from stress.

My stalker's mother was questioned, her statement recorded by the Becker County Sheriff's Department:

> She stated that he became very despondent and was obsessed with some girl. His mother stated she did not know what the name of this girl was, but she felt that the person must have been of some different nationality. . . . She felt that maybe it was his intent to come up here to kill this girl and then commit suicide . . .

Dad passed out flyers at work. He included the make and model of the car that he suspected was the stalker's—a Dodge Roadrunner, blue with a white stripe—based on information he gathered from the neighbors. The tip leading to the arrest was made by one of Dad's coworkers, who also happened to live behind our house.

My stalker was arrested and his car searched, the contents documented by the sheriff's department. Among the more mundane items—maps, Beary Bears fruit roll-ups, a paperback about Pearl Harbor—was what authorities would dub the "Rape and Murder Kit": cotton gloves, a shower cap, a bull whip, Vaseline, four tent stakes, rope, duct tape, a video camera and tripod, a hunting knife, one Rossi .38 Special with five live rounds in the cylinder, seventeen rounds of extra ammunition, and a shovel.

The stalker was jailed on one million dollars bail, and he stayed there awaiting trial at the end of January.

The trial happened to be scheduled on a day that was convenient for me—the break between interim and second semester. I had planned to come home from college and testify, but a last-minute plea-bargain entered the picture, and the stalker was put away on charges of assault with a deadly weapon, burglary, and illegal possession of a firearm. At the time, there were no laws in Minnesota against stalking. The trial was called off, and I never testified in front of a court of law. I never told my story.

Mom and Dad, disgusted with the gossipy, unhelpful attitude of their fellow parishioners, took their tithes and their casseroles and their Murphy's Oil Soap to another church—more than twenty years in the same church, where both their children had been baptized and confirmed, thrown out the window. They kept their nightmares to themselves and installed security lights on the eaves of the house. Not long afterward, they uninstalled them; the lamps flooded the yard with light every time a tree branch moved.

It wasn't until the following autumn that I cracked. I had decided to see the therapist on campus because, oh, I just wasn't happy. Couldn't figure out why. We were talking about my childhood or something, and then I started crying, and the next thing I knew I was in St. Joseph's Hospital, in the psychiatric unit, sans shoelaces, personal effects, and dignity.

Thus began a four-year depression during which I was in and out of hospitals and seeing therapists who mostly wanted to talk about (a) my issues with my parents or (b) my *feelings* about being stalked. Talking to an empty chair about feelings doesn't really do much for a person whose safety is still in jeopardy. Drugs—I've been on everything: Prozac, Depakote, lithium, Haldol, Wellbutrin, Zoloft, you name it. I was this close to undergoing shock therapy but decided not to out of fear that I would lose my ability to play the piano, my lifeline. It was then that I said *screw this* and found other ways to get better and stay that way.

About the time I decided to stop taking all that medication and to stop going to the therapist who liked to tell me about her other clients and who'd sometimes cry during our sessions, I came across a good book: *Trauma and Recovery* by Judith Lewis Herman. For the first time, I knew I wasn't crazy. I came to understand that what I had gone through was the psychic equivalent of terrorism, that there was a name for all those anxiety attacks, all the nightmares, the depression: Post-Traumatic Stress Disorder.

I had been diagnosed with all kinds of other things, from borderline personality disorder to schizotypic personality disorder, from major-axis depression to manic-depressive. But here, in my hands, was a shiny blue book that named what was truly wrong with me. If you can give it a name, you can look it in the eye and master it. Oh, and *it wasn't my fault.*

While he was being held in prison, my stalker became obsessed with a young female prison guard who had long black hair and a petite build much like mine. I'll call her "Lynn." He made sexual comments toward her and masturbated as he watched her from his bunk. Lynn quit her job, sued corrections for not protecting her, and won. After serving his full sentence, my stalker was released on parole, which he broke two weeks later. He was arrested with a shotgun in his possession and a piece of paper listing all the people he planned to kill, including judges, lawyers, and—first on the list—Lynn. Luckily he never found her house or her children inside it.

I was not on that list and neither were my parents. Maybe this is really sick, but I find it hard to believe that my stalker will ever forget me. I would like him to forget me, but I don't think it's possible: he hears my name and what he did to me over and over again as petitions are filed, hearings take place, and arguments are made.

Proceedings for his civil commitment have stretched out almost a year beyond his criminal sentences; during this time he has been held in either a state security hospital or prison. In the twelve years he has been imprisoned, there have been many times when he was almost released before another legal proceeding kept him safely locked away, sometimes with only hours to spare. I have learned to live with the way my stalker marks holidays and major events in my life with yet another hearing, another scare, another friendly conversation with a federal probation officer.

Lynn and I e-mail, wishing each other Happy Thanksgiving—hope we get good news; Merry Christmas—try to enjoy yourself; Hope you have a fun vacation—don't let this spoil it. She tells me to pray. I don't tell her that my faith in God, honed by years of church, family, and school, lies on the floor in shreds, like the tattered scraps of a garish, transparent costume.

Sometimes I feel a twinge of pity for my stalker. He has spent more than a third of his life in prison. I have hopes for him: to be completely rehabilitated, to visit his mother, to hold a steady job, to have friends, to have a normal life. I feel very sad for him, and then I make myself think about what will happen if he is ever released.

When that happens, I am not going to hope that God hears my prayers. Nor will I take any medication, wait for someone else to help me, or sit in front of a therapist and talk about my *feelings*.

I have bought a dog and a cell phone. I have learned to use a gun. The U.S. Department of Justice Victims and Witnesses Program has just sent me a recent Polaroid of my stalker: I can see that he has lost weight; he's a little less scary than before. I will send copies of this picture to all my neighbors, along with a short history explaining why they should watch out for him. I'm going to talk with my police department so that they don't bullshit around when I call 9-1-1.

I've signed up for a self-defense course. The administrator says that the instruction is aggressive and hands-on; men dressed in padded clothing and helmets act as aggressors, and the instructors show you how to kick the crap out of them, how to skillfully use the power of your woman's body. The best part about it is that they let you make up scenarios—situations you think might happen to you.

I'm going to come to class with my hair long and unbound. I'm going to ask them to turn out the lights, and I'm going to take off my glasses. I'm going to practice in the dark—blind. I will use the vibrations in the air around me to see him; I will finally trust my gut, no matter what other people say. If he dares to come for me again, he'll be surprised at how I've changed.

Look at how I've grown, I want to tell him. *Look what you've done for me. See? I am no longer afraid.*

Don't Worry
I Will Make You Feel Comfortable

A Monologue for Imagining

JANE, *Generically Asian, in her early twenties*

Standup comedy routine style. Black curtain, spotlight, one microphone, glass of water, stool, piano. An APPLAUSE sign behind Jane's head lights up on cue, causing the smorgasbord of Caucasians in the audience to laugh and applaud wildly. JANE wears a sad clown outfit, complete with whiteface make-up, baggy white jumpsuit, and pointed hat. Her demeanor is happy and energetic despite the costume. Lights up on JANE alone on stage.

JANE:

[*In heavy Korean accent*] Thank you for being here tonight! *Kamsahamnida!* It great for you to come in bad weather! In Minnesota, there are two season: road construction and winter. In tropical Korea, also two season: rainy season and dry season! [*APPLAUSE*]

That remind me, all time I stay inside because raining, I study calculus and engineering. *Aigo!* Say, I remember, how you know Asian girl break in your house? Your homework done and your dog gone! [*APPLAUSE*]

Yes, I am not lie! We eat the dog! We calling our national dish "bulldoggy." [*APPLAUSE*] But not any dog: we not eat ourselves, but our faces look like we've been chased parked cars! [*APPLAUSE*] Or should I say parked rickshaw? [*APPLAUSE*] *Kamsahamnida!*

How many you men here like Asian women? I see you at video store. Korean strawberry, chicken, people—small but taste good! [*APPLAUSE*] My roommate say Asian women tasting like peaches and smelling like jasmine. Lucky for you, there are ten thousand adopted Koreans in Minnesota—one for every lake. [*APPLAUSE*] We extra good because we come without lice or tapeworm. Almost pass for white daughter! I am honorary white person! [APPLAUSE] Ancient Chinese secret: No matter mail-order bride or mail-order kid— Oriental woman love you long time! *Kamsahamnida!*

I have designed this stage with Zen candles and feng shui from Pottery Barn! You like?

Thank you, you are a great audience. I want to singing a song for you.

[JANE *seats herself at the piano, takes a sip of water, and begins to sing while accompanying herself to the tune of "A Modern Major General."*]

I am the very model of a high-achieving minority
I got straight As and all white friends and even a sorority
I never bitch about my rights or blame my problems on
    the whites
I just work hard and sweep my shop and quietly grow
    erudite!
If I were ever discontent you'd never even have a clue
I aced my GRE, my TOEFL, and my catechism, too!
I don't cost extra money for the education bureaucrats
Because I don't complain about the culturally biased SAT.

[*Uncontrollable* APPLAUSE. *Piano still vamping.*] Hey I can't see you all there! I schedule appointment for eyelid surgery soon! [APPLAUSE] Maybe I get calves shave down too! And now I show you my very favorite trick! I play all Bach preludes and fugues at the same time, upside-down and backwards, while I kicking your ass in the ping-pong sport, with the one hand! Something else sideways, too—my vagina! Ai-ya! Me play joke! Me go . . . [*More* APPLAUSE. *Vamp back to "A Modern Major General," lights fade to black.*]

When winter arrives in Minnesota, the playing field of beauty is suddenly leveled. Buicks and BMW's, equally coated in salt, rust away one molecule at a time. Everyone looks fat in his or her coat and everyone's head is charged with static. All the women's legs remain unshaven and encased in thermal underwear; within snow boots, their reptilian feet *scritch-scritch* on their socks.

The semester I moved off campus was also the semester that I had to pay rent with real money instead of student loans and eat real groceries instead of cafeteria food. I bought my wieners, beans, and rice at the twenty-four-hour Rainbow Foods after work.

Bundled up, I was like any other Minnesotan—staticky, hairy, and lizardy. Definitely not sexy. Definitely not flaunting any skin besides that on my face. So what happened in the canned vegetable aisle was a real surprise.

He approached me by asking, "Are you looking for a job?"

If I hadn't been nearly hallucinating from exhaustion, if the fluorescent lights in the store were not surgical, if I hadn't just finished cramming for a test on *The Inferno* while I was supposed to be attentively translating pizza orders at the Deaf Relay—maybe the man would have struck me as more odd. But I answered his question.

"Uh, no. I have a job." I noted the man's dress—namely, he wasn't wearing a coat—and presumed he was a manager at the store and was looking for stockers.

"What if it paid fifty dollars an hour?"

I looked at him, wondering how anyone could earn that much money opening boxes.

"I'm pretty busy already, but thanks."

"It would be just once . . . are you familiar with caning?"

"Well, I've heard of it on the news."

"Do they cane people in your country?"

Still bemused, I said "no," irritated because here was one more white guy who couldn't keep his Asians straight.

"I'd pay you to come to my place. . . . Do you ever feel like you've been really, really bad? I'd just feel so much better if you'd punish me."

The light bulb in my head finally went on, and I said, "I'm not interested," and pushed my cart toward frozen desserts. I looked back and he had disappeared.

In the ensuing years, I've developed a highly sensitized Creep Radar, which tells me when I should walk faster, when I should cross the street, and when I should steer a girlfriend down the sidewalk the other way. This last radar trick, the ability to know—without turning my head—whether or not I'm being followed, is part of what psychologists call "hyper vigilance," a symptom of being traumatized— but I think it may be a side effect of being an American woman.

伍

Rules for Home Economics

One: Never waste. Two: Make things that are useful. A skillful wife can do both. A quilt is the perfect thing to make. Scraps of pants, jackets, skirts—old useless abandoned things—transform into starbursts and wedding rings, cabins, checkerboards, geese, baby's feet, or the unplanned plan called crazy.

What would happen if the pieces heard the echo of their names? Might they peel themselves from the new design to become a baby blanket, a stuffed rabbit, the things they once were? Would you recognize them with parts missing, jagged edges, threads that once bound them in artifice hanging like scars?

Months after he had arrived, four-year-old Tommy
told his mother that he had been reborn on the plane.
Had this been another birth trauma for him?

[THE CHILD WELFARE LEAGUE OF AMERICA]

Thump-thump. Thump-thump.

An unborn baby hears the strong, rhythmic heartbeat of her mother, and when the baby is born, the mother buys a little plastic machine that duplicates the sound of her own heart and hangs it on the railing of the lonely crib, to soothe the baby as the coldness of separation sets in. *Thump-thump. Thump-thump.* The crying baby falls asleep.

Funny how nobody remembers these sounds at all, how the background music of human transformation is lost in a pool of childhood amnesia on no particular day. Funny how, when I listen to one of those plastic heartbeat machines, the sound is alien and even frightening.

The roar of the airplane engine fades into white noise, a constant thrumming as I fall asleep somewhere over Alaska. The formerly energized tour group silently agrees on darkness and rest; the moms and dads and kids recline in their seats with thin blue blankets, close the blinds, turn off the overhead lights.

It is a long journey.

Thump-thump, thump-thump.

Children are brought to the United States and Canada
from Hong Kong, Korea and Japan in groups of five,
escorted by an adult. The children may not have a change
of clothing with them and some effort should be made
to help them look as fresh as possible when they meet
their new families.

[INTERNATIONAL SOCIAL SERVICE]

The crackle of the intercom breaks my fitful sleep; the pilot cheerfully announces our descent into the Kimpo Airport of Korea. The passengers slowly shake off their blankets and, one by one, snap open their shades. The window is equal parts sky and earth: green, terraced rice fields appear over my shoulder—the landscape of a movie, of people more mysterious than I.

The cabin fills with light; the continuous movie changes from *Stargate* to a Korean woman exercising. She's the kind of Korean woman I would come to love, the kind who says *Kamsahamnida* in a high, breathy voice and bows as gracefully as a dancer. She has the classic Korean face I can only describe as peaceful: there's something about the placement of the cheekbones; the eyes, just right; the way the elegant arch of the eyebrows suggests hard fragility.

She instructs the viewers to rotate their ankles and raise their arms from their seats to help get the circulation moving. I retrieve my make-up bag from underneath the seat and do my best to revive myself. How should you look when you meet your mother for the first time? Making myself presentable after fourteen hours on a hot, crowded plane seems impossible, but I do my best to at least look healthy: lip-gloss and blush, skip the dark eye shadow.

The earth pushes the sky out of the window, and as the rice fields give way to highways, I re-stow my carryon. Then the inevitable long taxi, the wait in the aisle, bags falling from the overhead compartments.

I would make this trip many more times. It was a trip I would grow to loathe for its press of bodies and its timeless, placeless quality—the feeling of being physically suspended in the eternal present.

I would not have made the first trip if it weren't for my college boyfriend, Shawn. He was everything I was not: he rode a motorcycle; wore a leather jacket and combat boots; twisted his naturally curly hair into long corkscrews; never met his father.

He also had the travel bug. He spent one of his high school years in India, learning how to eat beautifully with his hands and how to accept the kindness of strangers. He traveled to Katmandu during his stay, saw the Himalayas, endured the ancient process of tattooing with a needle and thread: his yin-yang symbol was exactly the size of a rupee. He developed an affinity for marijuana and a respect for the cunning of temple monkeys. In college, he spent almost a semester in Mexico before he got sent home with giardia, contracted shortly after he saw his first Aztec ruins. After graduation, he got the hell out of Minnesota. He moved to New York with his new politically lesbian girlfriend and their cat, did some lighting art at the Knitting Factory, gobbled a lot of Ecstasy, looked even groovier than before. He had that hungry artist look, a desire to consume more life, a fierceness I couldn't touch myself.

WHILE HE WAS IN THE ARMY, Dad had traveled to Hawaii and Florida, and when he and my mom were first married they vacationed in Florida together. Dad said he'd still like to travel, but Mom's system wouldn't allow it. Airplanes made her sick, and a sensitive colon made long car rides uncomfortable, fraught with fear of emergency and cold beads of sweat. A Folger's can and a roll of toilet paper resided permanently in the trunk, just in case.

By the time I entered their lives—my six-month-old body having been whizzed around the world from Seoul to Vancouver, Seattle, Los Angeles, Chicago, and then Minneapolis before being picked up and driven to Harlow—they had decided Minneapolis was the farthest they would go, and only in a case of absolute necessity.

WHEN MAKING PLANS FOR COLLEGE, I made my world as big as I could imagine. "With scores like this, you could go to . . ." I didn't hear the end of my high school guidance counselor's suggestion because the words meant nothing to me: schools out east or anything else east of the Mississippi were mere abstractions. But I knew about Minneapolis: home of Jimmy Jam, Prince and the Revolution, and Augsburg College—a Lutheran school founded by Norwegians— where my sister Carol had matriculated four years earlier. She would be the first member of our extended family to graduate with a four-year degree.

The majority of my high school classmates chose one of four

post-graduation options: the local vo-tech; the state universities fifty miles west in either Fargo or Moorhead; the military; the family farm. Attendance at a private, urban, liberal-arts school (and one belonging to the ELCA Synod!) was a clear deviation from the norm, an act of bravery and rebellion. Indeed, I had chosen a school at the very end of the known world, off the Riverside exit of I-94.

Shawn was born in a suburb of Minneapolis, so his world had always been larger than mine. His friends were all travelers, real Eurail veterans. His best friend, the son of a university professor, was half-Brazilian, spoke fluent Portuguese, and had married an ethnic Turk from Germany. (Her first name began with an "Ö," and not as an affectation.) We knew other people who had spent semesters abroad in Africa or who had come to college in the United States from Mexico, the Netherlands, Tibet, and France.

With the encouragement of all my friends, I gave myself a gift when I graduated from college. I signed up for the Children's Home Society Motherland Tour, which guaranteed hand-holding for the timid.

"Some people substitute outer journeys for inner journeys." When Shawn's mom spoke to me, she looked at me deeply with the same eyes that I loved on Shawn. She had noticed that I felt inferior about everything in general and a few things in particular; I was the only person in my circle of friends who had not traveled overseas. Her words were comforting, and she knew before I did that when I finally went to Korea, I would take my outer journey and my inner journey at the same time.

> *If sedatives are provided by the staff abroad, there will be*
> *a physician's instructions to guide you in their use.*
> [INTERNATIONAL SOCIAL SERVICE, 1968]

For my journey to Korea, I packed all the regular items: clothes for all kinds of weather, a photo album of childhood pictures for my mother to see, a good, borrowed camera, a blank notebook for writing, and my Depakote. The Post-Traumatic Stress Disorder was still a problem, resistant to talk therapy. What my psychologist could not fix with art projects was dulled by the endless supply of prescription drugs doled out by my psychiatrist. Depakote is supposed to level out the drastic highs and lows of emotions. For me, it simply erased them. The drugs drew a kind of surreal curtain over the whole experience, a sort of waterproof, third-person luster.

> *At the Port of Entry, Immigration may give alien registration cards (commonly called a "green" card) for permanent resident immigrants to the escort for safe-keeping.*
> [INTERNATIONAL SOCIAL SERVICE]

One step out of the plane and the smell of Korea hit me—the smell of a country inhabited by people who are not obsessed, as Minnesotans are, with clean, dry surfaces and disinfectant and whose culinary trademark is fermented cabbage.

Two lines: one for Koreans and one for "foreigners." I ogled the passports clutched by the Koreans, theirs just like mine, except with the seal of the Republic of Korea on the front. I had one of those, too, in the days before my name was changed from Jeong Kyong-Ah to Jane Brauer. For a few moments I stood in the rear of the room, wondering which line to join. Then, observing my travel partners' example, I correctly joined the foreigner line along with all the other Americans and said "thank you" in English to the Korean man who stamped my American passport with a Korean sixty-day tourist visa.

After passing through customs, we exchanged our dollars for *won*. The American moms and dads on the tour were particularly excited about the exchange rate; one thousand won were worth slightly less than a dollar, and they were looking forward to bargain shopping for Christmas gifts for all their relatives.

There were more "real" Americans than Koreans on the tour. Most were eager parents with elementary school–aged children, parents who had dutifully read all the literature about adopting a child from overseas and who had eagerly sent their Korean kids to Camp Kimchi for cultural education. Over the course of the tour, I would grow envious of these children whose parents were so enlightened. Many of them were not "replacement" children, as I had been, but children who were genuinely wanted for who they were. Their parents already had one or two children of their own, and because of their religious or social beliefs they "made room for one more" and welcomed a Korean child into their home. How I wanted parents like that, parents who wanted me for me, not ones who wanted me to act and look like their white child who had never existed.

I had come to Korea alone. Over the next five years, I would travel to Korea two more times, each time asking my American parents to join me and meet my Korean family. I knew how much my Korean mother wanted to thank them herself, to show them how grateful she was to have her children cared for. "No" was the answer.

"But you get two weeks vacation every year."

"We can't get time off work."

I didn't push it. It didn't matter that they would take time off work to sit on the deck in front of their house. They weren't going anywhere.

Many of the children who came on the tour were searching for birth parents. Their plan was to stay a week, see the sights, and conduct a high-speed search. However, I had already been in contact with my birth family for a number of years and our connection had been blessed by the Industrial Bank of Korea, my sister Eun-Mi's employer, which allowed her to use the fax machine for personal benefit. She and I had exchanged a flurry of faxes in the preceding weeks, arranging to meet at the airport. Then, I would spend the next week on the tour bus with the other Americans, and after that I would spend a week with my family in Seoul.

Along the walls, in the crowds, next to the baggage carousels— my eyes swept the airport, searching for my family. I saw no one that I recognized, and my heart sank. *Maybe*, I thought, *they hadn't understood my messages and had gotten the wrong time.* I slung my backpack over my shoulder and continued to walk with the group to the next station in the airport.

What a surprise when the double doors of immigration swung

open into the lobby. Banners, balloons, flashes, flowers. We were home. Welcome.

From the crowd, a beautiful woman in a white pantsuit—she was jaw-droppingly beautiful—rushed toward me.

"I am Eun-Mi!" my sister exclaimed and grabbed my arm, pulling me torso-first toward my family, all the while bouncing/shuffling in that urban Korean woman's walk, the Seoulite Shuffle, the result of wearing very, very fashionable high heels.

> *By the time they arrive—even those who have been able*
> *to eat, drink, and sleep—they are thoroughly fatigued.*
> *Some are dazed and apathetic, almost ignoring their*
> *new parents.*
>
> [THE CHILD WELFARE LEAGUE OF AMERICA]

Sitting here in Minneapolis more than six years later, trying to conjure up the moment of meeting my mother with only words on a computer screen, I can feel my mother's emotions of that day. Having known her, cared for her, heard her voice as she was dying—a voice that would connect me to her in the spirit world—I can feel her emotions now, without language. There are no words for these feelings.

But in the moment, I didn't feel anything, not my own emotions, not hers. My mother couldn't stop crying. She shoved a bouquet of red roses into my hands; she appeared frail, smaller than her five-foot frame.

The sky did not open up, the angels did not descend, the theme from *Romeo and Juliet* did not play. My half sister Sun-Mi was there; I thought she was my other sister, Myoung-Hee, for at least week, until the real Myoung-Hee showed up. There was a friend of my mother, whom I thought must be a family member but who wasn't; there was an interpreter in a blue suit, and I didn't know where he came from or who he was, either. Cameras flashing in shocking explosions, the appearance of the world through the afterimage on the eye, people crying, chaos in a language I didn't understand. Then somehow I was pushed onto a bus with my mother.

She wore black polyester slacks and a royal blue top with metallic embroidery, her good dress outfit. In the darkness on the hourlong ride to Hotel Sofitel, she clutched my hand tightly and didn't let go. There was nothing we could say to each other, since I spoke no Korean and she spoke no English. So she held my hand, and all I could think about was how hot my hand was, how small she was, how her hand was bony.

So, I thought. *This is my mother.*

There must have been other people on the bus, but I don't remember them. In my memory, we are suspended together in the blackness, all by ourselves, with nothing to say, no words to say it.

The pictures from our initial meeting, taken by one of the tour operators prescient enough to have a camera at the ready, reveal a face that is different from the one that had left the United States. Strangely, all the photos from the first trip show me with a markedly changed appearance that I cannot explain. Whenever I haul out the big photo album, friends ask, "Is that you?" My face is rounder than in the photograph taken at the airport in Minneapolis before I left. The expression is different. I became someone else.

When I opened the door of my hotel room the next day and found her standing in the hallway, dressed in the same blue top and black slacks, a familiar look on her face and a plastic bag full of little green-and-yellow-striped melons hanging from her tiny fist, I was irritated. I thought my mother understood that I would spend a week with the tour group, then a week with her. I wanted to set healthy boundaries—not that healthy boundaries matter for a mother who has finally been reunited (a politically incorrect word in the adoption world: "made contact with" is preferable) with her child after more than twenty years, a child she never wanted to give away in the first place. Umma continued to invite herself to my hotel at odd hours, often arriving late at night, bearing plastic bags crammed full of tomatoes and watermelon—far more than I could ever eat—and always tied with a sturdy knot.

The girls in the tour group were delighted. The few on the tour who were of junior high and high school age were "grossed out" by the special occasion Korean food prepared for us—either too spicy or too unidentifiable or, in the case of prawns, just plain disgusting. "They still have their faces on!" they shrieked over their box lunches. Benign vegetable matter was welcome, and they eagerly helped eat the fruits my mother brought me.

Korea began to teach me important lessons from the first day my mother arrived unannounced. My modus operandi was to plan everything down to the minute, all details included. Arrive at appointments ten minutes early. Never go to the grocery store without a list, even if it's only for three items. Write everything down and let everyone know where you're going to be and when. They say that in heaven, Germans run the trains. I suppose in the case of a shortage of Germans, the trains are run by Minnesotans descended from Germans.

I assumed that the tour of Korea with this group of Americans was going to be the same: planned, predictable. For the most part, it was. We went to all the sights described in the advertisements for the tour: the Korean Folk Village, where we saw traditional Korean arts and crafts; the royal palace with its ponds full of carp; an orphanage with rooms full of toddlers and babies, two to a crib, and another room full of mentally handicapped adults weaving rag potholders on plastic looms; a home for unwed mothers; an amethyst mine and jewelry store; Buddhist temples; and the DMZ, where the propaganda of North Korea blasted over the border via giant loudspeakers. As long as I was surrounded by Americans, everything was safe, scheduled, and predictable, even in Korea.

My mother made it her project to add some unpredictability. She could not have cared less that my plan was to spend an orderly week with the Americans and then hand myself over to her. No, her baby was in Korea, and she was going to see me every single day I was in Seoul, whether it was on my itinerary or not.

She injected herself into the ends of my days, and I would apologetically phone Mrs. Han, the only Korean-speaking tour guide, to translate. Mrs. Han would arrive in my hotel room a few minutes later, and we all sat on the edge of the bed, my mother nervously wringing her handkerchief, crying, and talking all at the same time, and Mrs. Han nodding quietly while inserting comforting words here and there. The Korean language being longer and more syllabic than English, I had to wait patiently for Mrs. Han to summarize after what seemed like an eternity. The payoff for waiting was small. Oftentimes, Mrs. Han would simply report, "She says she is a terrible mother, and she asks your forgiveness."

"Umma, Mama, I understand why you had to give us away. It was the right choice. You are a good mother. You do not need to ask forgiveness."

Mrs. Han translated my words to Umma, and Umma went on in another river of words I could not understand. I grew impatient; I wanted to know every word she said, yet Mrs. Han translated very little. I realize now that Umma probably said many of the same things over and over again, and that Mrs. Han was very gracious to listen to her story again and again, because I couldn't myself.

Those nights, I began to understand my mother's hard life. During the next two weeks, I would hear the same stories through different translators, Umma's will to communicate transforming each person into her mouthpiece. Because I understood no Korean, she played out her stories in charades. She spoke passionately, as Korean lends itself well to dramatic speech, with all its aspirated consonants that sound like wheezing. My mother would hang onto these sounds for longer than anyone I've ever heard. Later, if we could find another person to translate, she told the stories all over again, with the same gestures, and from these signs I came to know exactly what she was saying. She was a one-woman theater, five feet tall and one hundred pounds, full of fire and hot red pepper paste.

She told the stories to her friends who had heard them for years, to strangers she had never met before, to me. I think she hoped that this act of storytelling would redeem her, that through the telling people could see what she wanted to be and not what she had become. I wondered if she hoped that one day she would tell the story and the ending would magically turn out right, that she would have mastered her life through storytelling.

THE STORIES ARE CREASED INTO MY MIND WITH REPETITION, Umma's desire for me to know my own people suffusing each syllable. She told me how my father refused to believe I was his own and so threw me from the window, squalling, and how she found me dirty and sick when she visited me at the orphanage. She told me about the cold September day that she sent me and my sister to America, how she was so distressed that she forgot to wear shoes and walked through the airport barefoot, how her mind split from grief after we were taken away and she carried a dog on her back, as she used to carry her daughter. How the dog was stolen.

She showed me her breasts to tell me that she loved me and had nursed me. I touched her old woman's depleted breasts, as she asked. *Touch me here, where I gave myself to you. I made you with my own body,* she seemed to say. She showed me her thick scars, where my father had beaten her, and told me how her once beautiful face had become disfigured: my father bit off her nose.

She told me how she slept underneath a cart with her remaining daughters and went door to door selling food, my older sister Eun-Mi imploring strangers, "Please, uncle, will you buy my pancakes?" She told me of the terror my father inflicted, how they traveled throughout Seoul for fifteen years so that he would not find her and my sisters, would not have the chance to beat them again. How she could not divorce him because of her *yangban* class.

My sisters told me more stories, of how the gifts my mother sent to America for my American parents and for my sister and me were given at a time when they didn't even have enough food to eat. She had sent beautiful sweaters knit with her own hands, hanboks, a bamboo mat, jewelry. All these, my sister said, were bought with Umma's heart. They told me how, in times of Umma's greatest need, her friends turned their backs on her, and her stepdaughters betrayed her. And they told how things got better after my elder sister married and they were no longer alone in the world.

This woman—my mama, who made me and saved me, who loves me ferociously still—asks my forgiveness. I feel ashamed of my easy life, of my petty, bourgeois whining. At least I had enough food to eat.

At least I had a warm house.

Her stories worked their way through my skin and into my blood. I felt her bravery seeping in (was it courage or stubbornness that allowed her to live? or sheer drudgery?), into my own stories, merging with them, transforming me into her daughter.

I came to understand the beautiful, terrible culture of my mother, learned that her experiences were not so unique in a land where boys are more valuable than girls, where women carry the weight of duty on their backs, as they do their babies, so that by the time they are old they are permanently bent over, eyes to the ground.

I know you now, Mama.

First, the crack of lunch boxes opening. Then the cries of "Oh, gross!"— a duplication of yesterday and the day before, as the girls discovered yet one more black-eyed prawn with accusing hands tucked snugly in between kimchi and a rice cake.

I began to keep more to myself. I found a seat on the bus where I wouldn't be bothered and pretended to sleep. I recoiled from the group. Observing them observing the orphans, the word "zoological" came to mind, as it did when we visited the unwed mothers' home. Somehow, I felt that the American adoptive parents didn't quite see the orphans and the mothers as people but rather as interesting specimens, a menagerie of personified sorrow.

After visiting such places, there was group discussion, and although the adoptive parents showed such integrity and responsibility for asking me, I began to resent their probing questions. I was one of the oldest adoptees on the tour, so they thought I had answers for them and their children. *Look at me,* I wanted to yell at them during group therapy. *I am here alone and you are here with your kids. What makes you think I have anything figured out? I have nothing to give you.* My isolation grew in correlation with my jealousy of the younger children who had somehow managed to be assigned informed, involved parents.

In a country of Koreans, the Americans began to change in my eyes: normal-looking Minnesotans suddenly appeared too big, sloppy, pale. Their clothing seemed too comfortable, their shoes dirty, their way of sitting at low tables vulgar. I wanted to get away from them and their greed, the way they bought souvenirs in Itaewon, haggling and always calculating the bargain price in U.S. dollars. I couldn't stand the way the tour was like their *vacation*, the way it seemed that they could compartmentalize their experience of Korea into alternating intervals of group therapy and shopping.

At South Gate Market—the outdoor market crowded around the five-thousand-year-old gate of the original walled city—I saw my chance to slip away into the throng of black hair. I took careful note of where I was, then chose a straight street and walked quickly away from the tour group, past the orange vendors, the women squatting and sorting squid, the ropes strung high with leather purses. *Walk, walk, walk.* No one noticed. I spoke no words and blended in, undetected for at least an hour, enjoying my experience as a "real" Korean. The shoulder-to-shoulder density of the crowd opened up and swallowed me, welcomed me into a sea of people where I could be lost in the sameness.

Suddenly, everything seemed more real: edges were sharper, more in focus; colors brighter; sounds cleaner; odors more pungent. The third-person, waterproof luster that blanketed me in the tour group fell away: no longer *miguk saram* but *hanguk saram*: not an American but a Korean.

I saw women chop pork, cross-sections of snouts and cheeks steaming inside clear plastic bags, the aroma mingling with the music of a legless beggar, who slid himself through the knees of the crowd on a scooter, leather paddles bound to his hands, a blaring radio and steel begging cup strapped to his back, a human crustacean. Boys in black windbreakers shouted over skittering black centipedes; women sold frowning fish from plastic tubs the color of bubble gum; rice cakes nestled in rows as numerous and colorful as rounds of pastel make-up in a department store; leather purses hung high above imitation Ralph Lauren clothing, the polo club placed on the wrong side of the horse; dark, glistening ribbons of laver sat rolled like garden hoses; barrels of dried mushrooms to be boiled and eaten with

sesame oil lined the walkways, where I joined in the swarm of bodies and no longer stepped carefully to avoid the used wash water, the
residue of manual labor that seems to snake its way onto every
Korean floor, every sidewalk, every surface where shoes tread.

The tour guide disapproved. "You stay with the group," she rep-
rimanded me later. I understood that she needed to keep the tourists
together, that she would be in trouble if she lost any one of her
charges and had to delay the bus. But it felt good to be surrounded by
Koreans, good to know that I could take care of myself in my country, good to be a part of a people, the majority. So I kept looking for
opportunities to escape the Americans, my heart beating loud in
my ears with the anticipation of metamorphoses: the thrill of becoming Korean again, just like everyone else, alive inside the belly of my
motherland.

I recorded the end of the tour week in my diary: "Going back to
Seoul—second to the last day of the tour—Hooray! I wish I were
going back with the rest of them, yet I feel glad to be staying . . . I still
don't think I have a real feel for Korea. The bus ride to Seoul will take
five hours. Plenty of time to reflect on how scared I am to stay with
my mother."

It had been a week of bizarre juxtapositions: temples filled with
thousands of golden, compassionate Buddhas; the scene of the
orphanage, where the children who could lined up for military hair-
cuts and the five who could not because their hydrocephalic heads
were too heavy lay motionless on the floor; the moldy tunnels dug by
North Koreans past the border displayed as a tourist site; yellow
strings of dried fish hanging in a department store; dancers whirling
with pulsating peonies at the Korean Folk Village; exhaustion.

My roommate, who had been adopted at age eight and remembered the phonetics of written Korean but had completely lost her
ability to derive any meaning from it, confided, "Sometimes I don't
feel like I belong here." I thought it was an odd sentiment, but during
a dinner with her in a rural village in the mountains, sans the tour

group, it seemed the whole restaurant of people stood around us and stared as if we were bearded ladies. I finally understood what she meant and scribbled in my diary that night, "I belong more in Germany than Korea. At least I look like I don't speak the language and people will expect that from me. I don't want to come here and teach or study. I'm an American and that's where I belong."

When I came to love Korea, it was because of my family, not so much for Korea or Seoul itself.

The moon is disguised by streetlights. The scent of Kentucky Fried Chicken floats past the blue violin shop and around the corner, mingling with the sweet smells of the bakery, with its cellophane-wrapped jellyrolls and breads filled with bean paste. Down the side street, past the instant coffee machine and the noodle stand, groups of brown earthenware crocks filled with pungent sauce occupy every balcony and patio from street level up.

The streets are narrow and winding, a real feat for a car to navigate, never mind two going in opposite directions. Motorcycles and bicycles are more useful here, in the walled neighborhoods punctuated by fruit stands offering strawberries and striped melons. The walls, numbered in even intervals with paint or magic marker, show which apartments are behind each iron gate.

Inside apartment 1474, my American tennis shoes, their heels stiffly upright, rest among the slide shoes of my sisters and mother. From the narrow basement window, I hear the buzz of a motorcycle stop and see a man's feet walk past, to another apartment. My clothes, having been vigorously scrubbed on a wooden board, hang on a line in the kitchen stretching from the wooden toilet stall to a bit beyond the gas burner.

Umma busies herself preparing my bath. She squats next to the wall in her pink rubber shoes, first running cold water from a hose and then heating it on her gas burner in a stainless-steel bowl. The blue flames lick the silver bowl; steam rises from the center like the hands of Deaf people singing hymns. It is a hot night, so I don't mind sitting naked on the wooden scrub board that she has just used to wash my clothes.

The water heated, I motion to her that I understand what she wants, and I will bathe myself now. But no, she wants to wash me.

The blue gas retreats into its coils. I unfurl my body as Umma lathers up the soap in a little green scrubbie, almost the same sort of thing used on pots and pans in the United States. She scrubs. Hard. Years later, when I finally learned how to take care of my body, I found this same sort of exfoliating cloth in the Asian grocery and brought it home and showered with it, every morning remembering the night my mother made me clean.

The water is warm as birthwater. Umma squats, her legs turned out like a patient onion picker reaching through dust to find the smooth, satisfying fruit of labor, the daughter she believed lost. She washes me hard and quickly, with so much ardor it hurts, and I become a child again. I release my American shame of the body, let her lift my arms and scrub underneath and on my back and my legs, as she wanted to so long ago, as she had done the day she brought me home from the orphanage, starving and dirty. She needs to see that my body is well, that I have eaten good food and have grown healthy and strong.

Soapy coronets swirl into the floor drain, like the radish peels and toothpaste and laundry water of the day, in this room that doubles as kitchen and bathroom, in this basement apartment with no sink or shower.

I am naked, elemental. There is no pretense between us, no hiding, no shame.

She sees the tattoo on my back, something forbidden by my American parents. The ink had gone too deep and formed a raised scar, so even though I could not see it without the aid of a mirror, I could touch it and know it was there.

Umma does not flinch when she sees it. She understands this scar on her daughter, the alchemy of emotion made visible. It is a phoenix the size of my palm, its wings outstretched and its mouth open in song. The tips of the wings are orange and yellow, darkening to black as they reach the center of the body. In the center of the black body lies a small red heart.

It is on fire.

Umma pours home-brew from a teapot. It looks like the water left over in the bottom of the pot after the rice cooker has been on all day. She motions for me to try it, so I raise the bowl to my lips and taste. She and her friends burst into laughter when I squint my eyes and clamp my mouth tight.

I thought her friends had come to see me, an oddity, a lost daughter, a surprise. But the visitors who came in those late mornings and early afternoons did not seem very interested in me. Then again, what can you do with someone who doesn't speak your language, except examine her appearance and talk about her in the third person? Mostly, the guests came to pay their regular visits to Umma, who greeted them with wine and cut-up pear on a plastic tray.

Where was all the shame I had expected? Children's Home Society had deliberately prepared the tour group for disappointment. We were warned that many women do not tell their families about unwanted pregnancies; the shame for them is so great that often their own families do not know about the child who was given away. The missing child is never mentioned. So if the mother even agrees to meet her child, it must be briefly and in secret.

Umma's friends already knew the story. It was a story that she had told many times, to many people. Always in her memory, I was a ghostly but undeniable presence in her life—probably to the chagrin of my younger sister, Myoung-Hee. However, if Myoung-Hee did feel slighted she would never tell me; her Korean manners wouldn't allow her to disrespect an elder in that way.

The women seemed like old, old friends who were comfortable in each other's lives and homes. They didn't knock on the door when they entered but announced themselves with a shout as they descended the stairs, took off their shoes in the doorway, then let themselves in to the main room and folded their legs on the floor, chattering all the while. They dressed formally to visit, in pressed slacks and fancy blouses, always with jewelry and make-up. They brought watermelon, thin almond-flavored cookies, rice cakes to be dipped in sugar.

Umma, by far the most animated of the friends, gestures rapidly with her small hands, as if her enormous energy cannot be contained in such a small body. She spears pear with a toothpick, eats greedily, sucks her teeth clean, unbuttons the top button of her pants and belches. The ladies chat for an hour before they leave to attend to their own families.

"Umma is sanguine," Eun-Mi and Myoung-Hee announce after paging through the Korean-English dictionary. Perhaps this explained how she was different from others. She was not concerned with appearances, so she never wore make-up or jewelry; dying her hair a rich auburn color was her one foray into vanity. She was who she was, and you could take it or leave it. You could accept her—a woman who had run away from her husband and later divorced him, who had given away her children, who cleaned an office building for a living, whose emotions ran high—or you could leave her alone. The people she knew respected her, and if there were people around who didn't, I suspect she wouldn't have given them the time of day.

My cousin Ki-Sung was one of the regular visitors. That summer, he was still working for Samsung. When I came back the next year, after the Korean government pulled subsidies from companies, he was working as an importer of human hair for wigs, and four years after that, he again found work in the computer industry.

No matter what the temperature or the state of the economy, he dressed as a businessman, in a suit jacket, white shirt, and crisp pants. His patterned trouser socks were just as important to the ensemble as his tie.

Ki-Sung borrows a pen and paper from Umma and diagrams my ancestry.

"Men," he explains, as he draws a row of squares. "Women," he says, as he connects the squares to circles.

He explains that he is my grandfather's brother's grandson. *What?* Because of the difficulty with language, I'm not always sure who is related to me and how, and I'm sure I misunderstand often. What I can see is that Ki-Sung is a beloved family member, as are all the people on my mother's side, while those on my father's side are regarded with suspicion.

My uncle, who is my mother's brother, is also a beloved family member. He holds my hands and speaks to my mother, his voice full of wonder. He is a little brown and silver man, the male version of my mother, dressed in a clean white shirt and gray slacks, a leather belt, a shiny wristwatch. His gold-capped teeth match the gold of his eyeglasses, and although he looks like an important retired businessman, I do not know what his business was.

"Your mother's brother," Ki-Sung says, "helped send you to America."

I wonder if he was the person who bought her shoes that day in September, when she was so upset that she brought her children to the airport in her bare feet. She said she always kept those shoes as a memento of that day.

After my mother's death, I learned more about Korean customs, and I wondered why he hadn't adopted me. Although the practice was nearly impossible after the devastating Korean War and the period of industrialization that followed, it had not been uncommon at one time for extended family members to adopt children, in order to keep the bloodlines pure. Perhaps Uncle wanted to but couldn't because he feared my father, or his wife didn't want me, or, more likely, he could not afford to feed another mouth.

As Uncle talks with my mother, his voice shakes a little and he quickly wipes a tear from behind his glasses. I can see that he loves me and that he feels almost as much guilt as my mother. Before he leaves, he presses a stack of crisp paper won into my hand. I feel terrible taking money from this old man, but I realize that it is better to take it than to protest, for it is one way he can show me that he cares about me and that he wishes the family could have taken better care of me long ago.

Umma has few possessions; she has either by choice or by necessity avoided the American habit of having more things than one person could possibly use, things that are bought and stored "just in case you might need it." Everything she owns she either uses daily or keeps because of its great sentimental value. Her two-foot-tall statue of the Virgin Mary is one of these prized possessions, decorated with two rosaries and placed next to a candle.

"Your mother is Catholic," my cousin explains. "She converted five years ago from Buddhism."

Umma owns just a few changes of clothing, some thin towels, her bedding, a few dishes. Around her apartment, I spot things that I've sent her over the years—a pennant from my college, a crystal candle-holder, my graduation picture.

Half her black lacquer wardrobe is filled with bedding. The other half has a rod for hangers and a high shelf. From this shelf she pulls out a large cardboard box, which she places on the floor.

She begins to pull out family pictures, and I immediately recognize a copy of the same photo that I had brought to kindergarten for show and tell. There is a photograph of my American mom and dad that I had never seen and a description of them in English, from the child placement office. There is a letter that I had sent as a child, written on Garfield stationery. Here is the evidence that she was there all along; she wasn't a myth or a made-up person. She wasn't just a name on a piece of paper. She was a *real person* all along, a mother who saved things in boxes for the day she would see her children again.

She shows me pictures of my father and pictures of herself. Some of the pictures are burned on the edges.

"Your father," says my cousin, "burned these. Your mother took them away," he says hesitantly, "before he could burn them all."

Umma busily acts out the scene of pictures falling to the floor, saying "*Aigo, aigo!*" as she gathers up the pictures and stamps out imaginary flames.

She gives me a picture of my father to take home. He looks like a normal guy, not the stumbling drunk I thought he was. He is standing outside a house with a tin roof. Eun-Mi and Carol, then known as Mi-Ja, stand next to him. The pink flowers are in full bloom. Only one corner is burned off, part of the brilliant spring sky.

We examine the photographs and each other.

The physical similarity is striking. The ironic thing is that it should *not* be striking: physical similarities, as well as similarities in personality, are normal in most families, where people tend to look and act more or less like each other. But for us, it was a point of amusement and pride. We were amazed at how I fit into the family, and when Carol came to visit a couple of years after I did, it was the same amazement all over. As if our years in America should have watered us down. They didn't. We were still intact, still genetically family.

"Same-same," indicates Eun-Mi, who knows the English words to point out hands that are the same, as well as similar hair color, ears, noses, and lips. For personality characteristics, I say, "Me. Eun-Mi. Umma," and then go into a routine of exaggerated mock crying and laughing, to show that we are emotional. Then I say, "Myoung-Hee. Carol," and trace a straight line over my lips and make my face as expressionless as possible. Eun-Mi smiles, laughs, and nods her head in agreement, while Myoung-Hee remains expressionless, agreeing inside.

Eun-Mi says they recognized me the instant they saw me. It was the walk that did it. Each of the sisters has the same characteristic walk, to varying degrees, becoming more pronounced in relationship to the height of the heel on her shoes. "PICK up your FEET," my American mother used to say, and despite my very best goose-stepping, I always reverted back to my natural, shuffling, static-producing walk.

"We are sol-ry," Eun-Mi enunciates carefully in her classroom English, "we send you far away to Am-el-ica. It must be hard. No Korean people."

I hide my surprise by steering my eyes to my tennis shoes, eyebrows inadvertently forming two halves of a wide M.

Eun-Mi's brand of truth grows from instinct, not theory or academics. I'm not accustomed to unadorned truths like this.

The version of the truth I'm used to is the urban, liberal, Minneapolis brand. The brand of truth that is brandished by former hippies on the fifteenth re-sole job of their original Birkenstocks. The kind of truth that is the privilege of white, middle-aged policymakers, messianic in their bead earrings and Ecuadorian clothes, who can afford to eat organic every day and to buy recycled, cruelty-free everything.

The liberal Minneapolis brand of truth is colorblind, and it can usually be summed up on a bumper sticker. It says all it takes is love to make a family. Race doesn't matter. That is, until decisionmakers, laden with guilt, start counting the "people of color" in their organizations. "People of color" equal funding, a pat on the back, a reprieve from punishment by more important decisionmakers.

Like a true Twinkie, I had checked "white" in the box on all my college forms.

Real reason: I didn't want to be Korean. Korea was a place that couldn't be talked about at home; it made other children leer at me in school. Korea was the reason my face was mutated, why my glasses wouldn't quite stay on my nose, why it was hard to find clothes that fit. It was the reason some children weren't allowed to play with me, some felt justified in calling me a chink or a rice-picker, and adults didn't feel compelled to defend me.

Self-deluding reason: what is on the inside is what matters. I checked "white" because I was *culturally* white.

Every semester my little forms came back from the registrar's office corrected to "Asian-Pacific Islander." My liberal, diverse, private, Lutheran school invited me to all kinds of Pan-Asian events and stuffed my mailbox with offers for tutoring in the English language, oblivious that I was one of the few people who tested out of freshman writing and had matriculated on a full-tuition academic scholarship.

Faced with the choice of dealing with certain rural Minnesotans or with urban liberals, I'll take politically correct any day, but the situation is still uncomfortable, a little bit like having been raised by wolves.

I decide on my official version of the truth and look up from my tennis shoes.

"Don't worry," I say to my sister. "Umma did the right thing. I was happy growing up. It's no problem to be Korean in America."

My smile is exaggerated.

We are shopping for fabric in the market. We walk with small but quick steps through the shoulder-to-shoulder crowd; we may be jostled at any time by someone carrying a steaming tray of soup and rice on her head. The stalls are grouped by what they sell—Western clothes, jewelry, glasses, leather goods. All the hanbok tailors are on one floor, and we walk and point until we see some fabric that we like.

It has always been important to Umma that I know about traditional Korean dress. The first Christmas we were in the United States, she sent a box with hanboks for my mother and my sister, with a request that we take a photograph and send it back. Somewhere in a photo album at my mom and dad's house there is a Polaroid of Mom holding me, ten months old, with my sister next to her. They are wearing their hanboks and cat's-eye glasses. The photo never made it to Korea; Mom said it was sent back.

Umma checks the price with the tailor and decides we will buy from this stall. The tailor turns and asks me a question, and the look of confusion on her shiny face when I stammer, "I'm sorry, I don't understand," gives way to a kind nod when Umma immediately explains for me. The other tailors have heard, and they turn from their stalls and look at me, rudely, it seems, but Umma pays no attention. She doesn't care what other people think. She is buying a dress for her daughter.

This is how we pass in the market. Any time I might have to engage in conversation with a stranger, either Umma or Eun-Mi immediately gives a quick explanation, and that is that. There are no more questions.

I love them for speaking for me, for defending me so that people will not assume that I am either Japanese or retarded. They do not shame me for who I am and how I cannot speak or understand, nor do they shame me for the million faux pas I know I commit daily. They take care of me and love me unconditionally, because I belong to them.

I choose fuchsia fabric, the pattern typically Korean in that it is bright but balanced in a way so as not to be garish: gold and silver birds surrounded by swirls of blue, green, and violet, tails glittering with the joy of flight.

The stiff fabric will be sewn on to a more comfortable white lining to make a long, gathered *chima* that hangs from the armpits to the floor and is held to the shoulders with straps. A matching long-sleeved *chogori* with long ribbons to tie into an *otkorum* will be worn over the skirt. I try on *tanghea*, narrow satin canoes embroidered with flowers on the upturned toes.

"*Nabi*," Eun-Mi says as she touches a completed hanbok hung from the ceiling. She sees the puzzled look on my face and quickly refers to her dictionary. "Put-ter-pry," she announces as she waves the light fabric of the hanbok back and forth, the long ribbons dancing merrily next to the rippling skirt and wide sleeves.

I still look confused, so she hands me the dictionary with her finger on the English word.

"Butterfly," I say.

"Oh, but-ter-ply!" Eun-Mi says back. "Hanbok is like butterply."

Suddenly, it seems that we are surrounded by shelves full of butterfly wings, all waiting their turn to fly.

The dressmaker measures my chest and arms for the chogori and my height from shoulder to feet for the long chima. Then Umma beckons "*Kaja!* Let's go!" and we are on our way again.

I almost have to run to keep up with Umma, her whirring legs slicing through the black-headed crowd.

We scurry up the granite steps and through the narrow doorway of the jewelry store. The squeaky-clean glass cases are filled with gold and jade. Umma gives the jewelry clerk the usual explanation about why I don't speak Korean. The clerk, a polite young woman with a Chanel hairclip, regards me with a nasal "Oh," and a nod that must be pity.

"Choice-a," Eun-Mi says in her Korean accent, a high-pitched, little-girlish way of speaking that is infinitely sweet. "Mother buy"—she laughs in embarrassment; she doesn't often use English and she is unsure of her pronunciation—"jewelry for American Mother."

To my American ears, it sounds like, "Ma-tha buya jew-a-ly por Ame-lican-a Ma-tha."

I smile, then point and nod to some small, inexpensive items, but these do not sufficiently show Umma's gratitude to my American parents. She and Eun-Mi choose an enormous jade ring set in gold with cubic zirconia accents. The shopkeeper places it in a fuzzy pink box.

"Choice-a," Eun-Mi says again. "Tay—lo."

The way she says our nephew's name is like the flight trajectory of a paper airplane, the arc starting high and fast, then dropping quickly on the second syllable. We set about our task of choosing something for Taylor, our two-year-old, red-haired, half-Korean, quarter-Greek, quarter–undefined Euromutt nephew who lives in America with our sister Carol.

We choose a tiny gold ring, flat and round on the top, engraved with filigree. The shopkeeper extracts it from the case and stuffs it into a fuzzy pink box.

"Choice-a," Eun-Mi says again. "Ca-lol."

Although Umma will always call us by the names she gave us, my sisters, who like to practice their English, often address Carol and me by our American names. For me, this would change the third time I went to Korea, when I stayed for a month, during which my sisters addressed me always as "Kyong-Ah." But for now, when I could scarcely pick my name out of a spoken sentence, they called me "Jane" and my sister "Carol."

Last, we choose jewelry for me. I'm appalled at the amount of money that Umma is spending, but I know it would be rude to decline her gift. I choose small gold stud earrings and a chain necklace.

"No, too small!" Eun-Mi exclaims.

"I like it!" I exclaim back. I have started to speak English in a way that my sister will understand, complete with the high-pitched, nasal Seoul accent.

We bicker a little bit back and forth, until it becomes clear that I must choose something larger.

So, like a know-it-all, naïve college graduate who thinks she is going to be "alternative" and cool, like a dumb American who tries to mimic the native culture but fails badly without even knowing it—

I choose a gold, reversed swastika.

I thought it would be great to take back to America because it's a Buddhist symbol, and I would look super-exotic wearing it, and I was so happy with myself for even knowing it was a Buddhist symbol, and so on.

Eun-Mi's eyes almost fall out of her head as she gasps, "Ma-tha ees Cat-o-reek!"

I am completely embarrassed and don't even know how to apologize. So I have to content myself with my own internal monologue: *Stupid stupid stupid! What were you thinking?*

Eun-Mi and Umma quickly choose a cubic zirconia–encrusted gold crucifix, Umma gives the clerk a stack of won, and we rush out the door amidst bows and "*Annyong!* Bye-bye!"

We scramble down the street again, Umma faster than either of us in her good dress outfit, Eun-Mi in a navy blue dress and Seoulite-shuffle shoes, me with my American legs hanging out of my shorts and ending in my increasingly inconvenient, unfeminine, tie-on rather than slide-off tennis shoes.

"*Balli-balli!*" shouts Umma over her shoulder. "Hurry up!"

It came to me as other great truths do: from a voice I hear without my ears.

I had been at Umma's apartment for nearly a week, surrounded by the Korean language from the moment I woke to the moment I went to sleep. My Jon Hassler novel was my security blanket: I clung to it each night before I went to sleep, reading over and over again the descriptions of rural Minnesota and its English teachers and clergy. But by the end of the week, the Korean language began to permeate even my dreams.

The dream was plotless, a rehash of the day's sounds. Although I couldn't understand it, there it was—a full-fledged Korean language dream complete with Korean women talking and me having no idea what they were saying. And then something quite extraordinary happened: the dream seemed to dissolve, although I didn't wake. And what was left was a kind of heightened reality, from which there emerged a very loud voice that asked, "What is your name?"

And I said to it, "My name is Kyong-Ah. It never used to be, but it is now. My name is Kyong-Ah."

Home chef, the modern alchemist, starts not with base metals but old chicken hearts and livers, broken backs and flightless wings. Boil them; strain them. Extract the undesirable parts; accent the desirable flavors. Serve up consommé, chicken liver pâté with toast and apple rings, aspic in half-globes with carrot flowers suspended in amber.

Consider another recipe: Start with a girl whose blood has been steeped in Korea for generations, imprinted with Confucianism and shamanism and war. Extract her from the mountains. Plant her in wheat fields between the Red River and the Mississippi. Baptize her. Indoctrinate her. Tell her who she is. Tell her what is real.

See what happens.

Witness a love affair with freaks, a fascination with hermaphrodites and conjoined twins, a fixation on Pisces and pairs of opposites. Trace a dream that won't die: a vision of an old woman slumped on a bench, her spirit sitting straight out of the body, joined to the corpse at the waist.

陸

Dear Jane,

You are a brave young woman, keeping me alive. I am like a parasite; I exist only because you do. If you had not been born, I would have died.

People do not see me, although we share a heart, a face, a mind, and a body. You have the benefit of being the twin who is seen. Me—I must hide behind you.

Take care of me. Take care of this body because, you know, it is really mine. That face you see—mine. The hands you use to eat and work—those too are mine. You are living a borrowed life. Don't forget.

Kyong-Ah

During the time I struggled to hold myself together, Carol used Mi-Ja's body to pass Umma's genes to a child who would never meet her. Umma's grandchild, Taylor, was the son of a former football star and a go-getter mom who had achieved where Mom and I had not: Carol was pretty, popular, and smart—right from puberty. "You wouldn't get such good grades if you weren't such a slut with that teacher," Mom told her.

Through adoption, Mom had rescued us from the fate of becoming prostitutes, though our rampant sexual energy managed to surface anyway. "Does it itch down there? Do I have to take you to the doctor?" she exploded, shaking furiously in her polyester nightgown when she discovered her young daughters, aged four and eight, masturbating in their bedroom late one night. She was appalled and angered, a failure as a mother, her daughters having fallen into such carnal sin. Later, the mere thought of Carol experimenting with boys was enough to send her into instant prayer and housecleaning.

But no amount of divine intervention or Lysol Pine Action could save the elder daughter from her "wickedness." The Lutheran preacher needed to make a house call in order to get her back on the straight and narrow path. After all, the Kingdom of Heaven is as difficult for a person to enter as it is for a camel to pass through the eye of a needle. The good reverend made the house call and was not particularly alarmed, and so that put the martyr right back in the same place, with an ungrateful, devious, whoring sinner as her charge and with no recourse but the comfort of the church library. She checked out as many of Dr. James Dobson's books as she could and made sure she read her *Portals of Prayer,* which gave her a different, proper prayer for each day.

The same qualities that drew prejudice when Carol was young in Korea deflected it from her in Harlow. Her skin was lighter than mine, her eyes larger, her face less broad. Her eyelashes curled, her hair was almost brown and possessed the anti-gravitational ability to feather. Plus she was not too geeky, not too introverted: she was not too anything but wonderfully a little bit of this and a little bit of that, making her well liked by girls and boys alike. Smart enough but not bookish, a little bit athletic, a little bit musical, and four years older: she was who I wanted to be.

And, despite Mom's worries, she wasn't experimenting with boys. Afraid of what might happen if she brought one home, she only managed to date the son of the carpenter who built Mom and Dad's house; he was pre-approved and was over to fix the roof, anyway. Throughout her college years, though, she racked up five marriage proposals before she finally said yes to a coworker at her first job in the mental health field. Mom interpreted Carol's success in love as yet another sign of her manipulativeness, her success in her career as an indication of prolific ass-kissing.

Carol did not build her ordered life through guile, but through assimilation. Carol's assimilation was so perfect and complete that she didn't remember her own Korean name, didn't have an interest in

Korea, didn't have an interest in *my* interest in Korea, got married, moved to the suburbs, bought an SUV, had a baby.

And for babies we do things that we really don't want to. Like find out our medical history.

We hadn't talked much since the stalking and my subsequent depression. Frankly, I was not much fun to be around, and my behavior reflected badly on Carol, who by then was working in a hospital's psychiatric unit doing lockups and four-point takedowns. Then she called me at work one afternoon. "I'm going to Korea. What should I bring?"

A beautiful rosary for Umma, honey and instant coffee for Eun-Mi, a necklace for Myoung-Hee: these were my suggestions for Carol to buy and wrap, but I knew that I had received a gift from her as well. After many years of hardly speaking, we were ready to begin the unraveling—of who we were in our American family, who we were in our Korean family, and who that made us together.

As the story of her visit began to unwind at a faster pace, Carol referred to Umma as "our mother" instead of "your mother" in conversation with me. She had taken many years after her weeklong trip to claim Umma for her own.

"It was like I couldn't breathe, I couldn't catch my breath," Carol said about the moments when she saw Korea again for the first time. "I thought I would remember something when I saw Korea from the plane, but I didn't, it was just that tightness in my chest."

"Did you remember anything at all?" I asked.

"No. I thought I would. I thought when I smelled things or when I heard the language I would have memories, but I didn't. I couldn't believe I didn't remember places or people or anything. You'd think I would; four-and-a-half-year-old kids have memories—Taylor can remember things from when he was that old. And our mother was so mad at me! She couldn't understand why I didn't speak Korean, she was mad because I didn't like the kimchi that she said I used beg her to make; she had made some especially for me and I didn't remember it. And I didn't know how to use chopsticks, so she took them and flung them across the room."

Carol went on to describe her humiliation, not understanding anything and Umma trying to re-enact breastfeeding her, how Umma wanted her to stay and Carol was afraid that she'd steal the tickets from her and make her miss the plane, and then she'd be stuck there all over again. She had had American dreams long before Umma sent her away.

Umma had told me once that when our father beat her, Eun-Mi always said to her, "Let's run away together." But Carol always said, "I will save a dollar and go to America." She would always figure out where to go to get what she needed.

Umma became frustrated and angry with her American daughter, so forgetful, so unlike the daughter she once knew. Why couldn't she remember *anything*? So while she was in Korea, Carol found a friend in Eun-Mi, the older sister she never had (though Eun-Mi remembered her), who also had a husband, a child, and a mother-in-law. Carol admired Eun-Mi's relationship with Umma, that of best girlfriends, shopping together, sharing secrets, helping each other. This was the same relationship she longed for with our American mother but was more successful cultivating with schoolteachers.

It's all about where you get your love.

My new plan was to sleep only with men I had slept with before; that way, I reasoned, I didn't have to count them again. I spent New Year's Eve 1998 in an evening gown and feather boa, pushed up against a jukebox at the Triple Rock. The whole punk rock band was there; I was with the drummer, a friend from college who fit my new criterion. His friends nicknamed him "Frenchy," in honor of one legendary throat-excavating incident at First Avenue. The New Year revelry continued at the guitar player's apartment, where I watched the dateable members of the band and their girlfriends pass out one by one, face down on the brown shag carpet. The cats, accustomed to the smoky environment and comatose humans, stepped carefully through the living room so as not to disrupt the party.

When I received the call in February that Umma had a heart condition and was having surgery, I called up the French for comfort. He was busy paradiddling away on his practice pad and watching TV with the sound off. He was probably stoned, too, although he smoked marijuana with such regularity that it was hard to tell when he was messed up and when he wasn't; he was just perpetually relaxed. "Are you going to do the boyfriend thing or not?" I nagged. What I wanted was for him to drop his sticks and come over instantly, give me hugs and sympathy and hot tea.

It didn't happen that way, as a lot of things were not to happen the way I wanted. The relationship lasted only another four months before it became the latest installment in a series of failed romances.

I knew the relationship was really over the day we left to go camping in the Boundary Waters Canoe Area Wilderness. We had gone to the camping store, where I bought matching bandanas, cookware, and a sleeping pad. Then we went to his mother's house in the suburbs, where he submitted his parking tickets for payment and raided her pantry for food; he didn't have a lot of money since he had been living off unemployment for three months, during the height of the record-breaking Clinton economy. She gave him forty dollars for gas and whatever else he'd need. Since I was on my early-twenties self-righteous kick (I am an American, liberated, feminist, empowered woman! I am not going to be a sad sack or a victim. I define myself by what I *do,* not by what I look like, definitely *not* by what *happened* to me, and especially *not* by the fact that I was *adopted.* I have limitless energy. I am strong, independent, in control.), his behavior was rather, well, unattractive to me.

French's mom was so *nice.* All told, so was French. But, after my visit to Umma, his prolonged adolescence (okay, okay, maybe I was jealous) irritated me. Time weighed on me: I realized that Umma would not live forever, and her heart problem was yet another friendly reminder of my own mortality.

Umma had moved up in the world since the last time I visited her. She had a washing machine (but no dryer), a whole room for a bathroom instead of a toilet with a wooden box around it. She no longer had to heat water on a stove just to bathe: a box on the wall allowed her to choose gas for the stove, for the water in the bathroom, for the water in the kitchen, or for the *ondol* floor. You can't have everything all the time, as my American mother would say.

Umma looked fine, despite (or because of) her angioplasty. I walked with her to work, a couple of miles through winding back streets, and helped her clean the office building, gathering up bags of garbage and polishing the windows that were too high for her to reach: at five feet two inches, I was a good deal taller than Umma. My American mom would have been appalled: Umma mopped with only water, no disinfectant. There was nothing to clean with besides a wet mop, no wax for the floors, no Vanish for the toilets. So the office building had the appearance of cleanliness, but I wouldn't eat off the toilet seat like I almost would at my American mom's house.

My American mom would have been appalled, too, at the way Umma made fried chicken, heating the oil until it crackled and then tossing the chicken parts into the pan from halfway across the kitchen. Grease coated the stove and the floor and the walls. Umma left her rice soaking in the bathroom without a cover, left meat sitting at room temperature.

And, Mom would have been horrified at the way we slept together on the floor: Umma's hand curled tightly around mine, Myoung-Hee next to Umma, all sleeping together in the breath's rhythm: bliss. I never told her we did this: it would confirm that Korea really is a strange and savage place.

THIS TIME FELT MORE LIKE FAMILY. Whereas before I was rebuffed when I tried to help in the kitchen, this time I was allowed to help, even in making *mandu*. Umma rolled out the noodle dough with the side of a green *soju* bottle, and Myoung-Hee and I squatted next to the table, stuffing the wrappers with pork and vegetables. Myoung-Hee's dumplings were perfectly petite, the seams flawlessly pinched together, as cute as a row of new compact Daewoos. Mine were big, hulking things, too fat in the middle, edges colliding with each other like twisted bumpers, pork erupting everywhere. Myoung-Hee covered her mouth politely as she laughed.

As if not to overwhelm me on my first trip, no one had mentioned my half brother; I learned about his existence from Carol, who had met him during her visit. On my second trip, I met him, too. Umma, Myoung-Hee, Eun-Mi, her two children, and I rode the train south to Gimcheon, munching on dried squid dipped in mayonnaise, Burger King, and chocolates.

The train arrived late at night in Gimcheon proper. Then we took a bus up the hill as far as it would go, to Obba's little village. In the darkness, Umma and Eun-Mi tried to find Obba's house. *Crunch, crunch, crunch,* Eun-Mi scurried up and down the gravel road, her ankles intermittently twisting before she'd pop back up on the tops of her shoes. Now and then she'd argue with Umma, but we finally found the right street.

Or should I say path, or walkway? I don't think we have these words in English. It was a narrow maze of unbroken cement walls punctuated by steel gates, and behind the gates were tile-roof houses, and these houses were shaped the traditional way, with a courtyard flanked by one or two arms of an angular house. Obba's house, storage shed, and outdoor kitchen were behind one of these gates, but his barn was near the road, as was his truck, and his pear fields were across the road, and there were more fields crisscrossed with different raised-mud-road-things beyond that. The next day, when we walked by the intersection of the road and the path-walkway on the way to see Obba's cows, there were two withered old grandmas squatting, tossing four sticks on the ground: the ancient game of *yut*.

Here are things I like about Obba's house: two rooms for sleeping, an extra-warm ondol floor, lots of towels, and a hot water heater in the bathing and laundry area.

Here's the one thing I don't like about Obba's house in February: you have to go outside to use the bathroom. The toilet room is attached to the house, but it has its own entry. My nephew Sam-Dol showed his opinion of this arrangement: he simply dropped his pants and peed off the front stoop.

I know that Umma did not see her first child with any frequency after she left him with his grandmother; she is conspicuously missing in the important photographs from his life. And there was not exactly a coldness but a lack of familiarity between them that bespoke of a relationship more typical of nephew and aunt than son and mother. I felt a closeness to him instantly: although Umma had left him because her mother-in-law encouraged her to, after his father had died in the war, and she had left me because my father forced her to, we had Umma's absence in common.

Just as I must not call Eun-Mi by her personal name but rather by her relationship to me—*Unni*, a woman's elder sister—I must address Sung-Duk as *Obba,* meaning a woman's elder brother. I began to understand that in Korea individuality is not as important as it is in the United States, to such a degree that personal names are not used in conversation. They are useful only for written documents and for crowds: if you've accidentally dropped your sister's hand, you may need to use her personal name to distinguish your voice from all the other Korean women who've also become disconnected, each one yelling, "Unni!"

I learned Obba's personal name as we left the next day. He gave me his business card, one side printed in Korean, the other in English. I was sad to leave; I had quietly fallen in love with my brother, the dignified head of his household, who dressed in impeccable navy blue pants and matching jacket, spoke in a low, musical voice, and smoked with all the finesse of an old silver screen star. He was debonair even while eating fried chicken in his pajamas on the floor.

I like to think all kinds of things about him. For instance, that we both take the bulk of our genetics from the same grandparent—either Umma's mother or her father. (We hold the monopoly on bunions in the family.) Or that his father was the one whom Umma truly loved, and she was sorry she ever left Obba. Or that he likes me as much as I like him.

Some things I will never know; others I am learning gradually, with effort and determination. In the latter category are Korean manners and language, including the names of things with no English equivalents; Korean history; the difference between Eastern and Western dragons; how not to stereotype other Asian people. I am learning to navigate the gap in perception that lies between my view of the world, the white American view of the world, and the Korean view of the world.

Other things lie in the past, and it is impossible to re-create exactly what happened or to know what other people felt, especially when they have varying degrees of willingness to talk. There is a language barrier, and there is a cultural barrier. The cultural barriers are considerable; they divide Koreans and Americans; adoptees and adoptive parents; the religious and the secular; the givers and the receivers of social work. More often than not, I can only make an educated guess about past events, filtered through my own perceptions. The echo of an event leaves a trace whereby its form can be estimated.

How exactly did my American parents choose to adopt? What did their families think about it? Who wanted children more, Mom or Dad? How did Carol feel on the day she came to America? How did Eun-Mi feel on the same day?

My mom reminded me that on the day Grandma Brauer died we were at a wedding and came home early because Dad's sister called the church and left a message with the usher. When she said this, I remembered the absence of wedding cake that day; we left directly after the ceremony and before the reception. I could see the greeting line in my mind, and the real reason I sat in the hallway: because I had just changed my clothes. Now I remember the details correctly, I think, although the emotional moment remains the same.

Paging through my high school newspaper of senior year, I discover conflicting evidence: the majority of my ninety classmates voted me "Class Brains," "Most Likely to Succeed," "Most Original," "Biggest Overachiever," "Most Talented," "Most Creative/Artistic," and "Most Musical." Not bad, if those are things you value. But I didn't value my mental attributes; what I *really* wanted to be was "Prettiest."

One's concept of self is burned into the memory. I was fragile enough to let a few choice jerks—one group of guys who stuck together from junior high through graduation—pick away at my insides until there was nothing left. I didn't have the inner strength to battle them without any help from adults. I stood there and absorbed their hatred because—as Mom reminded me—"that which doesn't kill you only makes you stronger."

When I talk with other adoptees, I begin to appreciate the fragmentation of memory as it is distorted by the child's-eye view and the disruption of language. How are thoughts shaped by language? How do we create memories in Korean one day and memories in English, Swedish, French, Dutch, or Norwegian the next day? What people remember are dreamlike fragments that float in time, that have content but, strangely, no words: a command to look straight ahead as the mother walks away in the opposite direction; a flash of blue coat; a long hallway; a giant table of food that no one ate, the same table of food that left no memory in my American mother, who had never known hunger.

I have made it my task to reconstruct the text of a family with contextual clues, and my intent is this: to trust in the mysterious; to juxtapose the known with the unknown; to collect the overlooked, the debris—stones, broken mirrors, and abandoned things. With these I will sew a new quilt of memory and imagination, each stitch a small transformation, each stitch my work of mourning.

"*Unni!* Elder sister," Myoung-Hee says. "There is something wrong with Umma!"

The morning begins as all weekday mornings begin. Umma turns off the alarm clock at five o'clock and lies on the floor a moment watching her youngest daughter sleep. Myoung-Hee is a bit lackluster, too skinny and anemic, prone to boredom. She'll still be sleeping when Umma returns home from her job.

Lately, the walk has been harder. Her left leg has been giving her problems, probably due to her heart condition, she thinks. Perhaps she needs to have the angioplasty surgery again. And the dull headache behind her eye doesn't seem to go away.

Umma decides she had better hurry up if she's going to clean the whole building before the businessmen arrive. She gets up and folds her bedding, moving silently so as not to wake her daughter, then opens the wardrobe and sets her neck-pillow and quilt inside. She walks into the kitchen, closing the door behind her, and as she reaches for her clean work clothes hanging on the metal line, her left leg collapses and she falls face first onto the floor, knocking the breath out of her chest.

The floor is hard. A rivulet of blood makes its way from her nose to her upper lip.

"*Aigo, aigo aigo,*" she cries under her breath.

She flips over so that she is looking straight into the bare fluorescent light bulb.

She says a quick prayer to the Virgin Mary and crosses herself, noticing how the tile floor seems to steal the heat from her just-awakened body.

Umma instinctively massages her left leg. Her right hand vigorously pounds and pinches the wayward limb, but the left hand does not heed the command and remains on the floor. Umma tries to move her left hand again, but it won't respond. It lies there, upturned, relaxed. She tries to move her left leg.

Nothing.

She tries to move the hand again.

Nothing.

"*Myoung-Hee a! Myoung-Hee a!*" she yells, her sixty-eight-year-old voice lower and more gravelly than it was in her youth, when it was high and lilting, like her daughters' voices.

Myoung-Hee, who sleeps late and does not like morning, groans and puts the pillow over her head in the next room. The bedroom is dark, just a crack of light showing from the kitchen. It's not time to get up yet.

"*Myoung-Hee a!* Come here, Myoung-Hee! Come here, Myoung-Hee! Come here, Myoung-Hee!" Umma falls into a rhythm; she won't stop chanting . . .

Finally, Myoung-Hee appears in the doorway, her eyes half-open. "Umma," she whines.

Then she sees her mother on the floor.

The next few minutes are a flurry of gasps and *aigos*, with Myoung-Hee finding more strength than either she or Umma knew she had. Myoung-Hee picks up Umma—who is the same height as she but much heavier—from underneath the armpits and drags her back to the other room. She is suddenly very awake, and she wipes the blood from Umma's nose with a tissue and confirms after several pinches and hollered commands that indeed Umma's left side is paralyzed.

She reaches for the phone on the white doily and dials Eun-Mi.

Eun-Mi is already awake, preparing breakfast for her children, husband, and mother-in-law. She feels ambitious this morning, so she is cooking soup.

When the phone rings and she hears the news, she snaps into her very useful oldest sibling behavior. She evaluates the situation, asks her mother-in-law to prepare her son, Sam-Dol, for school, informs her husband that today they will drive to Seoul together. He must call his top employee at their store and ask him to stay there during business hours and handle the deliveries.

Eun-Mi quickly dresses her toddler, Young-Joo—who is usually unhappy for some reason—coaxing her along with smiles and songs. Young-Joo wears a red jumpsuit, and her mother quickly applies lotion to her face, singing while she howls, her tears taking off the lotion as fast as Eun-Mi can put it on. Then she wraps Young-Joo's hair in a tight ponytail on the top of her head, causing more screams and tears. Eun-Mi, unflappable, continues to sing her mountain and flower songs.

The trip to Seoul from Pyeongtaek, about seventy-five kilometers, takes about one hour by car. The highway and toll system in the northern part of the country is better developed than that in the south, so driving is a convenient way to travel, even better than the train or bus.

Eun-Mi moved to Suwon after her wedding. Her husband worked there with Samsung, and she worked at the Industrial Bank of Korea. When jobs became scarce, they moved, along with their children and her husband's mother, to a high-rise apartment in Pyeongtaek, an outer suburb renowned for its pears and rice, its green parks and enough space to drive a car. Eun-Mi and her husband bought a building near the outdoor market and decorated it in bright banners and fluorescent lights, announcing the opening of Pyeongtaek Electric. They sold appliances and electronics, ranging from refrigerators to CD players to rice cookers, and were successful enough that they were soon able to employ four other people. A table in the back and an added room with a heated ondol floor and a television made the store livable, so that the family could be there many hours a day, like a second home.

Now Eun-Mi, her husband, and her toddler are whizzing up the road, past the American military base, past the billboards and the water tower. Eun-Mi tries to rely on her husband for nothing, but she has never learned to drive and so needs her husband to take her to see her mother.

The maroon Daewoo minivan arrives at Umma's apartment amid a flurry of cries of "*Halmoni!* Grandmother!" and "*Eun-Mi a!*" Eun-Mi's husband stands outside smoking while the women's work goes on inside. Eun-Mi immediately decides that Umma must go to the hospital, so she and Myoung-Hee dress Umma like a doll, bundle her up in her coat, and cram shoes onto her feet. Eun-Mi, in big wedge heels and a tweed suit, carries Umma piggyback to the minivan, and the whole family rushes off to the Catholic hospital.

Dr. Kim confers with seven interns outside the hospital room. He is a large man, six feet tall and more than forty-five kilograms. His wide facial features and quiet bass voice give him a gentle appearance despite his unusually large size.

Dr. Kim flips on the light box and positions Umma's CAT scans, illuminating the black-and-white images of her skull and the upper section of her spinal cord. Because Western medicine is taught in English, Dr. Kim speaks to the interns half in English, half in Korean.

He points to a gray mass at the base of the skull.

"Here is the tumor," he says. "It is most likely cancer, but because it has metastasized so quickly and because of the location, it is too dangerous to confirm the diagnosis with a biopsy. The patient is paralyzed on the left side and has considerable difficulty focusing the left eye and suppressing the gag reflex. At this point surgery carries more risk than potential for treatment, and chemotherapy is not effective in reducing a tumor of this size. As you see here, there is also an infection in the brain and spinal cord. Therefore the best we can do is control the pain while we treat the infection and fever. If the fever breaks, we will release the patient at that time."

The interns nod in agreement. Dr. Kim dismisses them, and they depart as a single organism, like a caterpillar dressed in white lab coats, its percussive black shoes reflecting on the waxed and polished floor of the hallway. Dr. Kim glances once more at his teaching diagram of a healthy brain, places the CAT scans carefully into a folder, inhales, exhales, and taps lightly on the patient's door.

In the back of her mind, Eun-Mi knew that this day would come. She didn't expect it to come so soon: life had just started to become what it should have been all along. She and her husband were able to provide well for the entire family; Umma no longer feared her ex-husband after his death.

At the end of the day, Eun-Mi leaves Myoung-Hee at the hospital with Umma and drives with her husband and daughter back to Umma's apartment to find her address book. The next day, she will come back to the hospital alone, via bus, with a change of clothes and some toiletries, which she and Myoung-Hee will need for their extended stay at the hospital.

It is Eun-Mi's job now, as Umma's eldest daughter, to call all the friends and family.

Umma is dying. Come quickly.

Nine-thirty in the evening.

I am alone, making friends with solitude again, having moved from a large house in the suburbs to a one-bedroom basement apartment two months ago. My most current ex-boyfriend had swept me off my feet, bought a house, and requested that I live with him, all within a matter of months. He was everything that I thought I was looking for—gainfully employed (that was an improvement over the French), European, bilingual, tall, black hair, jewelry, spicy cologne, pastel shirts—the whole Latin man thing. I loved his stories about smuggling gasoline from Yugoslavia into Romania, bribing the guards with cheese, and about how he, as a student, had helped to overthrow Ceausescu and had narrowly escaped being shot. He had come to America by winning the lottery; good luck seemed to follow him everywhere. He managed to save forty thousand dollars in fewer than five years by playing the American stock market. Everything could be bought or sold, no big deal; he played the game well.

He gave me boundaries, and I liked it. It made me feel comfortable to know my place, "as a woman," he would say. I would soon find out that my place as a woman was a place without friends and with as little dedication to outside activities as possible. It was also a place that demanded unflagging devotion to my partner, devotion not to be averted for even a moment. If it were averted, he would find another woman who would serve his needs immediately; his way with women was not exclusive to me. He was jealous of the piano, and after he "accidentally" slammed the fall board down on my hands while I was playing, I knew I wasn't safe.

We argued. He blocked me into the bedroom. I cowered on the floor keening, making sounds like a wild animal, sounds I didn't know I could make and that I'd never heard before, uncontrollable sounds I couldn't stop. He said I reminded him of his mother. He took my house key and told me to get out, so at midnight I was on the road to Carol's house, driving past unlit store signs with only my purse and my hanbok in the back seat.

A few days later, I was in my own apartment, left to lick my wounds and wonder what went wrong. When would I get it right? Why had every romantic relationship ended in disaster?

I counted the names in my string of broken romances, obsessing over my responsibility in each failure. Failure. Failure.

Failure with men who were like my dad, failure with men who were the opposite of my dad. I failed brilliantly with men ages eighteen to forty, across all social and economic strata. I failed with writers, musicians, lawyers, salesmen, students, gas station attendants, retail workers, and waiters. There seemed to be no end to the line of men who could fall stupidly in love with me, and I with them, leaving both parties miserable in no time at all.

Carol had her own reasoning about all these failed romances; her bachelor's degree in psychology gave her just enough information so that she could diagnose me. "Reactive Attachment Disorder," she said. "Lots of adopted people have it. You have it and I don't because at least I had a chance to thrive before we were given up."

I researched RAD and ruminated on the lingering effects of PTSD and exactly how much of a mental illness alphabet soup I had become. Now, after a couple of months living on my own, I am considering the embarrassing but seemingly necessary step of attending an "Emotions Anonymous" group when Carol calls, providing a welcome break from my own thoughts.

"Hi, sis, what's up?"

"Eun-Mi's friend called me."

"What?"

"She has a friend in Germany. Her husband studied in the United States, so he speaks English. So Eun-Mi told her friend's husband to call me."

"What'd she say?"

"Our Korean mother is sick. Eun-Mi says to come right away. Can you go to Korea?"

"My God, of course I can! What's wrong with her?"

"She has cancer. She has brain cancer."

"Holy shit. I'll go. Are you going?"

"Yeah, I'm going for a couple of days."

"Let's go together."

"I'm looking for the best airfare online. Mom says she'll pay for the airfare."

"Really? You're kidding."

"No, I'm not kidding. She said she'd pay for it."

It takes thirty hours to travel to Seoul from Minneapolis, with layovers in Detroit and Japan and trains and buses and cars, which finally deliver Carol and me to the hospital—a sad, crowded version of an American hospital circa 1950. I had not slept during the entire journey; my heart was wrung with impotence. What could I do but come here?

I go to my mother's bedside. She is small, deflated, with tubes coming out of her, bruises on her arms from blood tests, collapsed veins, and misplaced IVs. Her left side is useless—paralyzed and blind. Her hair, vainly colored for years, has grown out gray with black ends. The thin hospital robe needs changing. The thick, humid air hovers like a canopy of sickness, diapers, and kimchi.

Eun-Mi turns Umma's head for her. She is trying to make her focus her useless eyes. She shouts something to Umma in Korean, which I do not understand. Speak at her loudly enough, and maybe she will be healed.

"*Cho ilumen Kyong-Ah imnida*. My name is Kyong-Ah." I practiced it on the airplane. I talk to my mother in the formal language of a Barron's diplomat training textbook. It is embarrassing, my poor Korean, my stupid words, my ability to inquire what time the train is coming, how much does this cost, and what is good to eat even though I cannot tell my own mother how my heart bursts when I see her. I am filled with shame.

She extends her hand for me to hold, disregarding all the tubes trailing behind. I lean close. In a weak voice, she says the only thing in English she ever learned: "I love you, Kyong-Ah. I love you."

I had seen cancer before. First in the bald head and haunted gray face of my neighbor, whom I adored as a child for allowing her husband to play tag with me and for sewing new button eyes on my stuffed dog. She kept orange candies in a covered dish. She smoked. She and her one lung took up occupancy in the guest bedroom of the house and received visitors in bed, smoking. Too late to quit now, what's the use, was the logic. My parents said, *It's okay, you don't have to wear your wig. Don't be embarrassed.* She wore her wig, anyway. The curtains were drawn in the living room, and the children were shooed out while the adults whispered a moment more. A filmy haze covers that day, a haze of smoke and resignation, of the confusion of children who don't know the end is near but who know that people are even quieter than usual.

My mother's mother had it, too, starting in the labia and moving out into her legs before the rural doctors noticed and sent her to University Hospital in Minneapolis. "I'm just like a manure spreader," she joked wryly as a nursed wiped her, her bowels having betrayed her violently. Later, as she drifted in and out of consciousness, her legs moved restlessly underneath the blankets, a macabre dance choreographed by pain. The next time I saw her, she was in her good pink dress from Sears, her jaw dropped too far back, her hair a little too tidy. Not the right shade of lipstick.

I had seen cancer at the hospital where I volunteered in the oncology unit every Tuesday afternoon. The sound of the piano drifted down the sterile halls, into the rooms of the dying, the hopeful, the bored. I played little pieces—easy Chopin preludes, Bach, old favorites. "Danny Boy" was the most popular: husbands and wives, emotionally decimated, gathered around the piano and sang the words, crying softly:

> And if you come, when all the flowers are dying
> And I am dead, as dead I well may be
> You'll come and find the place where I am lying
> And kneel and say an "Ave" there for me.
> And I shall hear, tho' soft you tread above me
> And all my dreams will warm and sweeter be
> If you'll not fail to tell me that you love me
> I'll simply sleep in peace until you come to me.
> I'll simply sleep in peace until you come to me.

Umma, I would bring you back to life with will and words if I could— pure words, crisp, fresh ones, like water and sky and air. These English words—transparent, swirling, full of light—I give to you, to imagine you into life again, because I miss you so, and because I cannot bear the thought of never seeing you again.

But to re-create you with the words of dying, the way I knew you the longest, suspended halfway between life and death—it hurts to remember you this way. Umma, I know that you want me to stop my sadness, you want me to let you go. So I will make you now with these words, these terrible, ugly words that I hate to write.

The words are the same in English as they are in Korean: morphine, massage, metastasized. *Same-same*. These are the words of your slow death.

"*Massage a julkaiyo?*" I asked you. "Do you want massage?"

The answer was always "*ne*." Yes, of course you wanted massage, and I rubbed your back, where you had carried me, trying to help your body drain the toxins. I rubbed your scalp, underneath which, just a half-inch away, your brain festered with infection and hallucinations. *Hasulri*. Delirium.

I came to know your body, each part of it, your nakedness never shocking to me nor embarrassing to you. I saw for the first time what you as a mother already knew: that I am made in the image of you; I am a daughter after your body and after your heart. Even if I fail to create you again with words, I will carry you with me, in the language of blood.

I had seen cancer, but not like this.

Carol and I stayed two days at a hotel, and then she flew back to America. I checked out of the hotel the same time as she, and moved into the hospital. Myoung-Hee slept with Umma in her bed, spooning around her and careful not to dislodge the IV. I slept on the vinyl couch across from them, part of the family unit but too fearful of hurting my mother to sleep next to her. I was afraid she would wake in the night and not know who I was.

Afternoons were filled with visitors bearing food wrapped in handkerchiefs. They set up camp around Umma's bed, turning the pullout kneeling bench into a buffet: fried chicken, kimchi, fruit. The sisters offered the guests miniature yogurt and ginseng drinks. The guests, dressed in their good clothes, talked loudly to Umma so she could understand through her morphine haze, through the weight of her tumor, the fever. She understood more than I. They shook their heads and spoke with Eun-Mi in the ritual of handing the responsibility of the family to the new matriarch. Eun-Mi seemed to grow in seriousness and duty, donning the mantle of care giver for both the young and the old. I was proud of her. My big sister knew how to talk with the doctors and the guests, how to keep Umma as comfortable as possible. Her words and her actions were filled with grace; the only tears she shed were outside Umma's room, her face turned toward the wall.

Umma, I imagine you the way you were—so frail, so scared—and the words stop. I'm sorry I couldn't do more for you. All I could do was help in the most mundane ways: put the covers on, take the covers off. Feed you. Tell you to swallow. Then pound you on the back when you choked. Wipe the vomit from your chin. Umma, every night when I go to sleep, I remember the soft, sagging skin on your hand, your brittle hair, the way your sweat soaked into your pillow. There was the smell of you, warm and tired, your palpable frustration, the way the tears ran down your face as you prayed, your tiny hands clutching your rosary.

I weighed your diapers, wrote down the numbers on a chart. Helped prepare the pine nut and rice porridge in your room, gave you medicine. It was the same every day, wasn't it? We waited for the infection in your brain to stop. How did we know if you were getting better or worse? By looking into your frightened eyes? By monitoring which language you spoke—Korean or Japanese? By counting the number of ghosts you saw?

Umma, if I could have given my own life to save you, I would have. How I wish I could have taken the illness from you, like the tree took the cancer from the queen.

Eun-Mi had taken Umma's address book from her apartment and called everyone in it. They arrived one after the other, true friends and fickle friends, relatives, relatives of friends, people thought missing for years.

On one of the eternal days, a husband and wife came with their grown son. The woman regarded me proudly, examining me, noting my plump cheeks. She was large for a Korean woman—stocky and muscular. Eun-Mi explained that this woman helped take care of me before I left Korea. I was at a loss for words in English, never mind Korean. What do you say to someone who risked the wrath of a crazy man—my father—who may have had to defy her own husband in order to take care of an infant who wasn't even part of the family? I searched through my memory for some glimmer of recognition, but as with my own Umma, there was no magical spark that made all the memories rush back. But she looked happy to see that I had returned to take care of Umma in her last illness. So I took a piece of her joy for myself, knowing that the defining event of my life had less to do with me than it did with other people.

Umma, I am afraid that if I write about you dying, someday I will finish, and then you will be gone from me, forever.

American hospitals are hushed and sterilized. All the conveniences are available, and the nurses do most of the work: change diapers, deliver food, administer medicine. Korean hospitals are noisy and packed; the elevators were crammed full of people each trip, and there were always more people waiting for the next elevator. The nurses did not bring food for Umma; we made it ourselves on a hot plate set on the floor. We slept with her and around her, keeping vigil through the night. We unwrapped the powdered medicine from its waxy paper packets and mixed it into her juice ourselves. We balanced her limp body on the toilet and sprayed her and the whole bathroom with water. The IV drips were made of glass, the nurses wore stiff white paper hats, the hospital became our residence.

I had never bothered to imagine what health care might be like outside America. So I was surprised when I learned that some things I considered standard were not standard in Korea: dry microwaveable body wash; ice chips; plastic pitchers filled with fresh water; sponges for the mouth; a portable toilet for close to the bed; extra linens. I struggled with my frustration; I knew what cancer care was like in America, but without these things to help me take care of Umma, what should I do? As always, I had to watch and imitate, like a child. All I could hope for was to be a help, not a burden.

The memories of that month are like still photographs, suspended without time. They surface like dolphins in the otherwise seamless boredom of care giving.

In my mind, I leaf through the pictures as if they were in a photo album. The brilliant colors of tourist Korea have settled into the hues of the everyday.

In this photo, we fold Umma's pink quilt at her old apartment, preparing to move her into a new apartment closer to Eun-Mi's home, one with glass in the panes of the sliding doors. In this photo, a deliveryman springs off his motorcycle with Chinese food in a metal box; we'll put the dirty dishes next to our shoes for him to pick up later. In this photo, a strong young man walks up the cement stairs with a green tank of oxygen on his shoulder; he sets it horizontally on the verandah, and we run the tube inside to Umma's lips; she thinks the oxygen mask smells bad. In this picture, I prepare tuna sandwiches for my sisters to taste; they screw up their faces the same way I do when they offer me roasted silk worms.

Here is the day we decide to take Umma for a picnic. We dress her warmly, and I carry her piggyback to the car in the parking lot. I set her carefully in the back seat, arranging her arms and legs, the door still open. Myoung-Hee is trying to maneuver the wheelchair into the trunk, but she can't get it to fit inside, so I tell Umma to wait and go around back to help Myoung-Hee. The wheelchair is almost in when we see Umma fall sideways out of the car, but we fail to catch her before she hits the pavement, face first, with a sickening thud.

That day we parked Myoung-Hee's Kia a half-mile away from the park and walked, lifting the wheelchair wherever the sidewalk abruptly dropped off into the street. We found a spot on a hill amongst the trees and ate *kimbap*, feeding Umma spoonfuls of yogurt and wiping her face as she vomited it back.

Her body was rejecting food, preparing to die. Every day when we changed her clothes, I noticed how the skin hung from the bones; her body—in recent years plump and matronly—had by subtraction taken on the look of my own—thin and spare, with the hip bones jutting out past the belly and the ribs outlining the chest. To see her dying was to see her first transform into me; to see her dying was a premonition of my own death. Although I harbored a secret wish that she would die soon, to save her from yet more wretched suffering, her thin body, which looked so much like mine, filled me with a determination to live my own life well.

The body of my mother—which I could carry on my back, lift to the toilet, dress, and roll over because it was so much like my own—was a stark contrast to my American parents' stature: big-boned Americans, both of them, my father more than two hundred pounds, my mother probably in the one-sixty range. How would I ever take care of them if they became ill? I joked with them when I got back from Korea, admonishing them never to get sick. I said it light-heartedly, but inside I worried, as I still do, about how I will care for someone twice my size and how I will integrate the American way of caring for the elderly and sick with my Korean experience, which seemed so much more honorable than shutting the ailing away in a nursing home or paying a stranger to do the work.

I wanted to be better than a nurse. At the hospital, people who came to visit Umma said, "You are lucky to have these daughters taking care of you." Eun-Mi was there whenever she could take the time from her store; Myoung-Hee was there constantly; I was there for the month; Carol came for a day and a half, before she had to go home to her own children. Obba had visited with his wife, and my half sister Sun-Mi—my father's daughter—also came when she could.

But the distinction of being a daughter did not necessarily help me take better care of her than a stranger would have. At least a Korean stranger would have been able to understand what she wanted.

It is after Umma's three-hour morning ritual: wake up, take medicine, go to the bathroom, wash, eat, throw up, wash, dress, go back to bed. Eun-Mi is at her store, and I've encouraged Myoung-Hee to go outside for fresh air and exercise. Umma and I are alone.

She sleeps on the floor, pillows propping her up to prevent her body from simply collapsing in on itself. As usual, I'm studying Korean, copying useful words from the dictionary into my notebook, practicing my penmanship as Myoung-Hee had taught me during the long hours at the hospital. I have almost mastered the alphabet, making me nearly on a par with my three-year-old niece. I am thinking of the vowels in order: *a, ya, o, yo* . . .

Umma wakes from her sleep talking in an excited voice, but I can't tell if she is in a delirium or not. I try to comfort her in the same way one comforts a child: try different things until one works. I massage her head—no, that's not what she wants. I adjust the covers—no. I bring her water to drink—no. I turn her over and rub her back—no. I take the oxygen away—no. I bring her food—no. When I take off the covers (by now she is nearly yelling; where did she get the strength to do that?) she pulls her paralyzed left side along the floor by her right elbow, in animal desperation, and reaches for the phone. She dials frantically and without luck: she only reaches the friendly, repetitive voice of the operator recording. Now she is screaming for Eun-Mi, for Myoung-Hee, even for Sun-Yung, the other stepdaughter who refuses to visit. "*Sun-Yung a!*" she yells in her guttural voice. She pulls herself to the sliding doors on the verandah and screams into the parking lot for her daughter, "*Eun-Mi a!*" I pull her back and close the door tight; what if someone were to hear her, and how would I explain? She reaches for the phone again; this time she has pitched sideways and landed on my lap. We are engaged in this struggle—me trying to take the phone away from her, she clawing the floor, the operator looping obliviously—when Eun-Mi walks in the door and I finally—too late—realize what Umma needs as we are both suddenly warm with urine.

In the old days, Umma had kept a careful tally of words I knew: tired, hungry, full, bathroom, airplane. She would have said *hwajang-shil* to me, and I would have known that it was the *toilet* she needed. But now, with the tumor pressing on her brain, she could no longer play these word games with me. She had probably said a variation on the idea of having to go to the bathroom, not just the simple noun I knew, and I was of no use to her.

My frustration and my disappointment in myself must have shown, because not long after that, Obba brought me to his house.

In my brother's manner of elegance, we buy tickets at the train station.

The train station is a clash of old and new. The building is completely modernized, with lighted signs and sleek ticket counters, but the heating is poor; large black stoves filled with coals chug away in the middle of the station, attracting those with rosy cheeks and cold, stiff hands. Old men and women in traditional dress squat on the floor, while teenagers dressed in tight black jackets sip coffee from vending machines.

Obba speaks not a word of English, but on the train to Gimcheon he talks to me in Korean and makes dates and drawings in my notebook, labeling them with *hangul*. I practice what is beginning to be my most useful phrase: *Mianhamnida. Mula.* I'm sorry. I don't know.

I would understand two years later, when I unearthed the same notebook and painstakingly looked up the words in my Dong-Ah dictionary, finally having enough language skills to be able to use it. On a map of Korea that he had sketched, he had labeled Gimcheon, Pyeongtaek, and Seoul. And beside the map he wrote two dates: October 12, 1954, 20:00—lunar birthday. June 25, 1950—War.

Gimcheon is about forty-five kilometers northwest of Geochang, where my mother was born, and one hundred five kilometers southwest of Pyeongtaek, as the crow flies. But distances in Korea become twice the distance they are in the prairie of western Minnesota; the mountains do not allow a straight road. We pass beautiful houses and high-rises and shacks, burial mounds and gas stations. We pass through Daejeon, where my grade school pen pal lived as a missionary. We pass things that are nameless to me. We pass onion fields that I had once seen ablaze with fire to clear the first harvest, now lying empty, waiting for the spring planting season.

It is a time of dormancy, of waiting.

While the air in Pyeongtaek smells of urban dirt—insidious gray street dust, grime on cars—the air at Obba's house smells of earth: caramel-colored cows, pear trees, dark clay soil. Obba has invested in something new since I visited him last: a litter of puppies—purebred, no doubt, since they all look exactly like their large, sad mother, but I've never seen this kind of dog in the United States. Obba is raising them to sell as food.

The practice of eating dog meat is probably as repulsive to Westerners as keeping cats in the house is to Koreans. The Korean government cracked down on dog-soup restaurants before the Seoul Olympics, relegating these establishments to back streets and decreeing that their signs must be posted in Korean only, not English. I thought it was an old practice that had been abandoned, but here was a bitch and her litter staring at me from behind the bars of a cage similar to a rabbit hutch. I shoved a hand through the bars to pet the mother.

My brother disapproved and made motions that I interpreted as "Don't touch! You'll contaminate your hands."

"Miguk e, mikuk saram sarang ke, ke kada hakkyo, ke chingu." I am trying to say that in America, Americans love their dogs. Dogs even go to school. We think dogs are our best friends. The literal translation of what I've said is "America in, American person love dog, dog to go school, dog friend." My brother excuses this mutilation of his language and acts out the Korean sentiment toward large, meaty dogs: he makes violent kicking motions in the air against an unseen dog, curses it out. The sight of my reserved brother participating in No Words Theater makes my sister-in-law and me laugh until it hurts.

Hyongsu, my brother's wife, has a broad face, thick hands, and a southern accent that even I can distinguish; the placement of the vowels is not nearly as nasal as that of Seoulites. It is her job to tend the family farm, and she has grown thick and strong with the manual work. She teases my slightly built brother because his job at the Korea Highway Corporation only requires him to drive the highways at night, looking for stranded motorists.

Unable to speak a word of English, Hyongsu resorts to children's games.

Ma, she says, pointing to the cows.

Ma, I repeat back.

Check-check, she says, pointing to a nuthatch.

Check-check, I say.

Cokiyo! exclaim Hyongsu and the rooster.

Cokiyo!

Mung-mung! Mung! She points to the dogs.

Mung-mung? I ask.

Mung-mung! Mung-mung! she barks enthusiastically.

Woof-woof! I tell her, because I can't even begin to believe a dog says *mung-mung.*

Woof-woof?

Ne, woof-woof!

Woof-woof! she announces.

Obba shakes his head in disbelief.

LIVING WITH MY BROTHER, HIS WIFE, and their two teenaged sons for a few days was a welcome respite from care taking. I woke to the voice of the neighbor's rooster identifiably crying *cokiyo* each morning; the smells of the kitchen as Hyongsu prepared the family's breakfast of soup, rice, and pickled vegetables; the whirr of the blender as she concocted Obba's liver tonic of yogurt and aloe vera plant. Sometimes Obba and I walked amongst the shrubby pear trees, which he had carefully trimmed in a way that at first glance made them seem mutated but upon further inspection showed buds evenly spaced two inches apart, so that the pears would all hang evenly, without disrupting each other. He demonstrated how he used bamboo rods to prop up the trees for correct growth and showed me the small stream that provided water for the fields. Amidst the pear trees and the backdrop of the mountains was a stone path that led to a shrine hidden behind a fenced courtyard. The little building seemed out of place, like a vestige of a greater time. I wondered who had built it—was it one of our ancestors? But I couldn't find the charade to make an inquiry of such complexity.

Despite Hyongsu's fabulous, painstaking cooking; my delight with my brother and my two charming, handsome nephews; the visitors, both friends and business partners; the women's picnic that my sister-in-law organized at a Buddhist temple, my thoughts remained with Umma. I was morose.

It was arranged for me to return by myself and meet Myoung-Hee at the hospital in Seoul. I would ride the bus in and meet her at the station, just a block from the hospital, and then we would run an errand at the pharmacy.

Hyongsu packed a pink handkerchief full of pears and a beef bone for Umma's soup and tied the top into a handle. I carried this and a heart full of thanks with me onto the bus, and at the last moment I couldn't resist turning to hug my brother. Such an American gesture: my brother didn't know quite what to do. So I also bowed, saying "thank you" in his language, and took a seat near the front. The bus pulled out of the station, and we waved good-bye as the bus turned the corner.

Myoung-Hee met me at the station, and together we purchased Umma's medicine at the hospital. It took only four hours of waiting in lines for approval, first in the emergency room, packed with moaning patients without curtains separating them for privacy, their hurting bodies exposed for all to see; then another line outside the emergency room, where Myoung-Hee paid with a thick stack of won; then in a remote corner of the basement, where the medicine was dispensed. We drove back to Pyeongtaek on the expressway and resumed care taking.

In order to dispense Umma's six medicines at the proper time and in the proper combinations each day, Myoung-Hee and I devised a system of labeling using only capital Roman letters and Arabic numbers. Each of the waxy envelopes was labeled with the code, and this made it easier for me to help. With the exception of the morphine, we administered Umma's medicine by the clock. The doctor instructed us to give Umma as much morphine as she wanted but to stop when her breathing slowed: it could relieve her pain, but it could also stop her breathing.

"*Ipun eggi.*"

Umma and I are lying on the floor. I have propped her up the way she likes, the same way I sleep: a round pillow underneath her neck, one pillow between her legs, one pillow between her arms, a quilt on top. I have opened the sliding door a crack and arranged her so she can see the strawberry truck outside. She is stroking my hair. "*Ipun eggi,*" she says again.

I imagine that in her delirious mind it is 1972, and she is forty years old and I am an infant. She has given birth to me, her third daughter—not a shame or a disappointment to her, not an investment or an expense, but a source of love. She kisses the baby's head and pats her on the back, holds her tightly against all the things that seek to harm her. The baby gazes back at her with all the love she has, for her mother is all she knows in the entire, vast world: she doesn't even know that she is separate from her mother, for she has been carried inside her for so long, and when she blinked her eyes open in the stark world she was cold for only a short time before her mother bundled her up again against her body. *Ipun eggi,* says the mother. Pretty baby.

I wish I could join Umma in her mind, so I could give voice to that tiny baby, tell her how much I love her. I want to enter the sad story that she remembered for so long and change its ending to something happy, change it into the fairy-tale life she dreamed of when she was only a girl herself, when she still had a mother. Most of all, I want to tell her that with her two words—*ipun eggi*—she has changed the rest of my story: I have never felt so wanted or loved, and this will be my deep well of strength, beginning at this moment—here, now, with her.

Sanakji. Small live octopus.

Eun-Mi is suddenly animated by the sight of a truck across from the video store. She discusses the price with the man in the blue work clothes and hat, and then he reaches into the tank in the midsection of his truck, produces an octopus from his net, and deposits it on the tailgate. The octopus is pale gray and moving. The man's knife is swift and sharp. He slices the octopus lengthwise, extracts all the organs and the nervous system in one piece, and discards the mass into a bucket on the ground. Then *chop, chop, chop* on the board he slices the meat into bite-sized pieces. The little tentacles are white and they're feeling around for something to suck on to. He quickly picks up the pieces and closes them in a Styrofoam container, which he in turn wraps in a plastic bag, along with a cup of red pepper sauce and some disposable wooden chopsticks. As we turn to leave, I look into the bucket, where the man threw the inside. It's lying on top of the other insides from earlier in the day. It looks like a little torpedo, self-contained in one piece, breathing in and out, the dilated black eye staring straight up into the sky, still living.

On the way home, Eun-Mi instructs me to hold the bag while she goes into a store to buy Jinro. She places it on my lap. I think I can feel the octopus trying to escape.

Ten minutes pass and we're back at the apartment. My half sister Sun-Mi, who comes to take care of Umma when she can, is already there. We make a circle on the floor next to Umma, who is sleeping. Eun-Mi unwraps the dipping sauce and the wooden chopsticks, then opens the box. The pieces are still in there, moving a little more slowly now, but they are startled into movement again when touched by a chopstick. Eun-Mi pours me a shot of Jinro, and it tastes strong and good as I chew through a tentacle, still moving.

Sometimes it was like watching a movie of myself: the tops of two feet in high-heeled slides from the perspective of five feet above, shuffling down the sidewalk, then a sharp turn to the left, up a stairwell. Gray, dirty stairs. Camera zooms out, revealing the feet attached to a person and Umma riding her daughter's back; the stairway, narrow and steep; Myoung-Hee walking behind. A glass clinic door at the top of the stairs. Camera shakes as daughter struggles to balance the paralyzed woman and open the door at the same time. Camera pans the small clinic, seizes upon a chair, turns to the opposite wall, lowers two feet, turns back to the chair, where the old woman is now sitting. Medium close-up of Myoung-Hee speaking with the receptionist, but no sound. Camera pans the wall opposite the mother and drops two feet; close-up of feet and floor from five feet above; camera zooms out from feet but is still focused on them; feet begin to walk. The floor is shiny. Enter an examination room. Repeat up and down procedure of taking Umma from piggyback. Camera pans room; reveals dirty yellow-white walls with a Snow White mural over the examination table. Enter nurse, catheter and rubber gloves in hand, a tray, a plastic bucket. Medium close-up of Myoung-Hee speaking with nurse, but no sound. Close-up of tray on the floor. Four Korean faces in a room. Camera pans to Umma, naked from the waist down, lying on the table. Close-up of Umma's eyes, upside down. My hands enter the frame, massaging her head. Close-up of nurse's hands. Sound of rubber snapping. Quick frame of catheter being inserted. Umma wails. Pan from Myoung-Hee massaging Umma's belly to Umma's right hand holding mine. Close-up: two identical hands entwined. White knuckles.

Before we moved her from Seoul to Pyeongtaek, Umma had said, "I want to live thirty more days with my daughters. We will not work. We will only play."

The cancer had been quick, striking her down in only days, and the thirty days she wished to play turned into hourless days of sleeping, of idleness. I found it amazing that a disease that could take away her health so quickly could also allow her to live such a long time in limbo, balanced between life and death.

It was as if she had been a beautiful sailing ship, skimming along rapidly when suddenly she was deposited in a place with no wind, no movement. I could hardly feel her breath on my cheek as the morphine took away both her pain and her oxygen. Her lips were often parted in the expression of a deep sleeper, her eyes closed, watching pictures from another time.

During those days, the silk shroud was delivered in brown paper and made to wait in the armoire; its little pouch would hold Umma's fingernail parings, so that she might enter the new world whole. But we were still greedy for life, demanding her—forcing her—to live.

We daughters yelled at her, fought with her. "*Samkyo!* Swallow!" We made her eat, made her take her medicine, made her. "*Hebba!* Do it!"

Yet no amount of yelling, furious medicating, and reprimanding would bring back her health. Treating her like a child wouldn't retrieve the health of her youth; we kept her immobilized—living, yet not living.

Centuries ago, European ships bound for the New World were sometimes caught in a place without wind near the equator, the horse latitudes. On the southern side of the equator, sailors called the place the Calms of Capricorn, on the northern side, the Calms of Cancer. It was here, after days of the sun hot and vertical, the water and supplies dwindling, that sailors, in desperation, threw open the gates of the ship and pushed the horses overboard in an attempt to lighten the heavy load. The crash of flesh hitting water, the screams of panicked horses, the crack of men's hearts breaking as they drowned their loyal steeds—how their chests must have heaved when they made the decision, and how they must have rejoiced when that first, gentle puff of wind filled the white sails and pushed them from the stagnant place. The horses and the daughters, abandoned in the water, eyes rolling with grief, grow smaller and disappear as Umma and the ship sail their finer course, beyond reach, beyond sight, into the wide horizon.

The sky is black. On a long stretch of beach, two women and a child run up and down the sand. Around the curve of the harbor, the lights of Busan twinkle, a thread of glitter against the Sea of Korea. The wind is brisk and chill, so the child is wearing the woman's jacket, too large, like a game of dress-up. Now they light fireworks that they bought in a blue-and-white-striped hut on the seashore, and the pink and orange sparks shoot up into the cold night sky, bedazzling us, enchanting us into a few moments of forgetfulness. Shouts, laughter.

In these moments of happiness, I take my last photograph of

Umma. There had never seemed a time that was appropriate during the entire month, until now.

Her face peeks out from the pink blanket wrapped around her head and shoulders. The flash, too bright, illuminates every wrinkle, every last detail against the silhouette of Busan, that fishing village turned Asian Las Vegas. She looks to the side, not seeing me.

"Umma, look here, *yogi*," I had coaxed her, and clicked when I thought she saw me. But in the photograph she is already far away, already in another world.

We had come to Busan after I made my decision to go back to America.

The phone rang one day, and by both mistake and miracle the voice on the other end of the line had an American accent. Myoung-Hee, sleep-deprived and not really listening to the words, gave the phone to me. She thought it was a friend from America. I answered, and the Korean words were incomprehensible to me, so I stammered in English that I was sorry, I didn't understand, *mianhamnida, mula*.

Upon hearing me speak, the other voice broke into English.

The Church of Jesus Christ of Latter-day Saints was offering English classes in the neighborhood and was making calls to recruit students.

I had been thinking for many days about all the things I wished I could say to Umma but couldn't because of the language barrier. My fear was that I would never be able to say the things that would put both her heart and mine at rest.

So, when Elder Beauchaine called, I boldly asked if he would be willing to come to our apartment to translate. "I certainly want to pay you for your time and donate to your mission," I said.

He arrived with a friend at the appointed day and time. Myoung-Hee and I cleaned the apartment and made a tray of fruit and drinks, and Eun-Mi returned from her store soon after they arrived.

Black trench coat, white button-down shirt with a black tie, black pants: Elder Beauchaine and his friend were the genuine article— fresh-scrubbed Mormon kids from Salt Lake City, hardly out of their teens, serving their missions in the world before they went back to the States to complete the rest of the plan: marriage, children, and another mission for God when their own kids were grown and they were middle-aged.

In the meantime, they had been in Korea for almost a year without going home, bound to their promise to live as the natives do, and they were homesick. Their American fantasies were the same as mine: mashed potatoes, long, hot showers, pillow-top mattresses, elbow-room.

They were more interested in discussing the photo albums of their families and girlfriends than the religious literature they had brought. My atrophied English surprised me; over the month, it had become habit to express thoughts in lagged time: each idea revised into either charades and the simplest English words possible or one of the few Korean words I knew. If neither worked, as was most often the case, the thought was simply abandoned.

Their Korean, which they had learned in an intensive spoken-language-only Mormon boot camp, was mostly geared toward proselytization. So although they would probably not be able to discuss politics or science in Korean, they could discuss the love of Christ and, consequently, love between people. For my purposes, that was just fine.

We sat next to Umma's bedding arrangement on the floor. She was flat on her back, and I stroked her damp hair as we talked.

The day she took her children to the airport to say good-bye, so many years ago, there must have been one last moment, one last call before the stewardess took me and my four-year-old sister from her. And in that moment—which began to constrict like a spotlight collapsing into a pinpoint as the gate agent waited impatiently for the weeping mother, as the voices over the intercom announced last call for boarding—she would have wanted to say many things. Words to keep me safe, words to guide me, words to remember her by. The right words. It was those same words I searched for but could not find then, as I said good-bye to Umma.

"Please tell my mother," I said to Elder Beauchaine, "that I love her very much."

I picked out the word *sarang* and knew that Elder Beauchaine was translating my thoughts.

"Please tell her that she is a good mother."

I tried to find words for all the things I had ever wanted to say to her. Here was my last chance, and I knew it. But words failed me; how could I express the weight of my sorrow, give her the forgiveness she craved but didn't need, and say good-bye, granting her freedom—all through a stranger, all at that moment?

"Please tell her, 'Don't feel guilty. You are a good mother. You made the right choice.'"

Umma mumbled; her eyes were open, searching.

"What is she saying?"

"Something about you coming next year and having a big party. She says she'll make a lot of food." Elder Beauchaine had a puzzled look on his face; it was obvious there would be no next year.

"Do you think she understands what's going on, or do you think she's hallucinating again?"

"She's talking to someone named Sun-Yung right now. She's telling her to do something . . . who's Sun-Yung?"

"She's my half sister, my father's daughter. No one has seen her for years. She didn't come to visit when Umma got sick."

We stopped and watched Umma babbling away. She was not coming back.

"Umma," I said. "You've done a good job raising your children."

Elder Beauchaine translated, although Umma was talking to a ghost. It was clear that she no longer knew I was there, so that freed me a little. But I still groped for the right words that wouldn't come; I could say only awkward words that seemed so trite, so meaningless.

"You are a wonderful mother. But you don't have to stay here for us. We love you, and you can go. Don't worry about us anymore. We love you so much, and we don't want you to suffer anymore. You can go now. Don't feel bad for us. Don't feel guilty. You're a good mother. We love you."

Umma continued to hallucinate.

I looked at my sisters; all three of us, even Myoung-Hee, sat with faces contorted and tears streaming down our cheeks.

"Eun-Mi," I said, "I think she doesn't know my face anymore. So I think it's time for me to go back to America."

Eun-Mi nodded her head and quickly consulted with Myoung-Hee. Elder Beauchaine translated, "Your sisters would like to take you to Busan to see the ocean before you leave. You will go tomorrow."

The Mormons stayed a little bit longer, then left without accepting money for their mission or their services. Eun-Mi said it was a miracle that they came. Indeed, it was.

The next morning, we waited until Myoung-Hee had washed at the public bath house, and then Myoung-Hee, Eun-Mi, and Eun-Mi's daughter, Young-Joo, piled into the minivan with Umma lying down in a makeshift bed in the back. We were going to drive to Busan and back in the same day, to see the ocean.

But with road construction and Koreans literally having to move mountains in order to make a road, it took a whole day just to drive there. Myoung-Hee and I took turns driving, trying not to make any sharp turns or hit any bumps, as these would cause Umma to immediately moan. Eight hours and four rest stops swarming with American servicemen later, we arrived in Busan, deciding we would have to find a hotel and stay the night.

We found a vacant room in the top story of a hotel overlooking the sea. Despite the logistical nightmare of moving a paralyzed woman, a toddler, and three adult women from a bumpy parking lot, over curbs, into an elevator, and down a mazelike hallway, we managed not only to accomplish this but also to reverse our steps and leave the hotel room in search of food.

The beach was dotted with little striped huts selling sashimi. We chose a large tent with fish swimming in tanks near the entry. The heated tent was large enough for a dozen customers, but we were the only ones there. We lifted Umma out of her wheelchair, up the small steps, and underneath the flap of the tent, placing her on the floor next to us at the low table. We spread out floor cushions so that she could lie down comfortably.

The sashimi came out Korean style—with sodas, peanuts, salt, radishes, hot tofu soup, and kimchi. Eun-Mi, with her discerning taste, said it was not as good as it could be, but I thought it was wonderful to eat on the beach, so close to the sea. Umma could eat nothing, though we tried to feed her. She spent the evening on the floor, retching into a plastic bag. Eun-Mi remained surprisingly cheerful, seemingly at home with the contradiction of eating an expensive meal by the sea while simultaneously holding up her mother's cold, sweating face so she wouldn't choke on her own vomit.

My admiration for my sister grew as I saw how great her responsibility was. She cared for her own children and husband, her mother-in-law, her mother, our little sister, and me. All these people depended on her, yet her smiles were irrepressible and genuine; she laughed at herself and her crying daughter and our moaning mother.

After dinner, we walked the beach, and it was then that Eun-Mi, in a celebratory mood, decided to buy fireworks. It was her indomitable spirit that I saw light the sky that night, streaking up and then showering down, her way of being joyful despite bearing scars on her body even thicker than Umma's. Nothing—not our father's abuse, not poverty, not the indifference of those who allowed her to grow up without innocence—could ever extinguish the kind of beauty and courage that is the essence of Eun-Mi, my elder sister.

We made vows to each other to keep in touch and for me to visit again, even though we knew Umma wouldn't be there the next time. By doing this, we acknowledged that more than one person bound us together, that we were a true family with many members.

When Myoung-Hee dropped me off at the airport's curbside check in rather unceremoniously, I thought how good it was to be dumped off just like part of the family instead of being a foreign, honored guest needing one of the long, histrionic group good-byes that we used to have, when no one was sure if I would ever return. As I watched her little white hat inside her little white Kia speed off down the street, I thought how good it was to feel protective over someone, my little sister, perched on the cusp of adulthood.

I was sitting on that same cusp.

Surrounded by infants who somehow found the energy to cry during most of the fourteen-hour plane ride home, there was no sleeping, only thinking and remembering. I had learned some important things in Korea and made a list in my notebook:

1. Self-soothe.
2. Trust in people who love you.
3. Don't go back to men who are bad for you.

One of my last nights in Korea, my sisters and I stayed up late talking about men. The original man in our lives was our father, and Myoung-Hee and Eun-Mi sat on the floor talking about him next to Umma's diminishing body. They had begged her to run away from our father, and sometimes she did. "So why did she always go back?" I asked.

Eun-Mi understood me, and I could see her strategizing how to express her thoughts in English. After a moment she simply said, "Food."

I wondered if Umma really believed her children would starve without her husband, or if "food" was Eun-Mi's symbol for something larger—the condition Umma had grown into, in which she was completely inextricable from her abuser and returned to him time and again, giving him innumerable second chances and jeopardizing herself and her children. By the time she gathered enough courage to leave him forever, in a rare act for a Korean woman of that era, she had already lost two daughters, half her nose, and her youth. Because Umma kept forgiving, Eun-Mi bore wormlike scars from one of Father's beer bottles; Uncle's life had been threatened; Umma had been shamed by having a husband in prison; and she had given birth to one more daughter, who, in Father's undying hope for a son, was registered with a boy's name. (Duk-Chon officially changed her name on the family register to Myoung-Hee when she was twenty years old.)

We spent time talking about other men: how Eun-Mi's husband had to work too many hours at the store, and she missed him; how Myoung-Hee was always fighting with her boyfriend but also didn't want to date anyone else. "I hope then that my eyes me not choosy," she spelled out on a piece of paper after using stick figures to diagram her dating life from 1996 to 2000.

I tried to explain in the most simple way I could my own situation, which was that I had, in the days before I left for Korea, kind of but not really become embroiled with a brilliant orchestral conductor who was divorced in the United States but was sort of still married in Belgium, but by his account he and his wife/ex-wife were completely through with each other, and he was only helping her out at the moment because her mother was sick. This is how I learned two new words on the same day: *chuntchu* and *kechashik*, ex-wife and son-of-a-bitch.

When I returned to America, I slept for three days. Said brilliant conductor turned out to be a kechashik, as predicted. But it was through him that I met Mark, who would become my husband.

Dear Umma,

My boyfriend takes good care of me. He has a Ph.D.; he's a computer programmer; he's going to get a big raise at the end of the year. We live in a large apartment, see lots of movies, go out to eat, drive new cars. We only fight about one thing: food. Every week I plan our menu according to what's on sale, clip coupons, buy rice and beans and cabbage, a little fresh meat, eggs. We never waste anything. I try my best to make beautiful meals with leftovers, dressing up yesterday's food with a new spice and combining it with one new ingredient. He gets so frustrated with me—he wants to eat new food, he wants only certain combinations of food, he'll eat only certain things.

I think I absorbed things from you while in your womb, Umma. How else can I explain it? I get so angry with him—I forget that we could eat new food every night, that there's enough money. I forget that we don't have to eat every scrap, that food is plentiful, and that I might as well feed him what he likes instead of what is inexpensive.

It must have been the saddest time in your life, when I was in your womb and your husband grew more drunk and more crazy each day. You must have been filled with worry and sadness. I must have absorbed these things from you—I try to keep busy all the time, to forget about the worry and sadness that fills me no matter what the circumstance.

I have heard that some children are born knowing certain pieces of music. Because—for instance—his mother was a cello player, and she was practicing a certain piece throughout her pregnancy for an important performance, and when the child grew up and also became a cellist and finally decided to play that certain concerto, he was surprised to find out that he already knew it: an elegant fingering and bowing was already in his muscles, and the concerto simply poured out of him, though he could not remember ever hearing it before.

What did I hear, Umma, when I was in your womb? I heard the Korean language, and maybe this is why my tongue wraps around the words so easily, although I cannot understand what I say. I am babbling in Korean, like I did as a baby. My words are frozen in that place, an infant's language, an infant's comprehension.

But even without language, through the amniotic fluid and the faint light coming through the walls of your belly, I understood the brute emotions of fear and hunger. I absorbed them, made them part of my body, made them part of my life's fabric, so that I would go out and find men like my father, so that fear and intimidation and love became the same experience for me.

I dated men like my father without ever having known my father. They were flashy, glamorous men; men with a girl on each arm who spent money as a show of masculinity. Men who beat you when you gave your heart to them, who had something evil living inside them. Men who were handsome enough to get away with it.

When Mark came along, I didn't notice him. He was modest, a bit skinny and unhealthy-looking, but nice. My friends encouraged me to date him. "Give him time to make himself attractive to you," they said. So I did.

I heard your voice one afternoon in May. It was after I left Korea, a few weeks after you no longer knew my face. I was with Mark, sitting on my couch, hands cupped inside his like a tulip bud. He told me stories of his hands, how he had earned the marks on them: the calluses on the tips of the fingers built from twenty years of bass guitar; the mark above the right index finger from a car's moving belt; the absence of a fingerprint on the left middle finger from a deli-slicer. I noticed how olive-colored my hands looked next to his.

We had known each other for months, but we had only begun dating. He was shy as a deer, *sempre sotto voce*. The frequent silences were not awkward; they surrounded us like a warm sea, where I suddenly could open my eyes and see clearly without glasses, where I could hear his voice amplified, where each of his movements became a gentle current, pulling me in tandem with him.

It was then that I heard your voice so loudly. I heard without my ears. Your voice sounded from inside my head, filling it and pushing outward. You said, "*Nampion.*"

All my muscles contracted. I stopped in midsentence and looked for you. You were not there, but I had heard you clearly, saying this strange word I didn't know.

After Mark left, I looked it up in my little blue Korean-English dictionary. *Nampion* means "husband."

Umma, it is now more than a year later. Last weekend, Mark spent an hour on the phone with his parents in New York. He asked for their blessing, so he may ask me to marry him. They said it's a wonderful idea. I'm glad they agree with you.

We are making plans. I know that you approve, and that you have helped me avoid your mistakes. Thank you, Umma.

Myoung-Hee was finally connected to the Internet and experimented by using different names as sender with the same e-mail address, concocting combinations of her birthday and words that might be found on Korean T-shirts, such as "lovegame." Sometimes she wrote in English, other times Korean, and I would spend the next week decoding her words. I deciphered boredom, a wish to go outside and breathe fresh air, more boredom.

Finally, late in November, "gangsterjeong" wrote, "Today Mama die. My heart break."

And mine, too, both for my own sadness and for my little sister, who was yet unmarried, whose only job since the angioplasty had been helping Umma. Myoung-Hee had only a high school education, and she couldn't marry and have children until after her boyfriend's elder brother did. What would become of her now? Would she live with Eun-Mi in her small apartment, overflowing with two children, a husband, and a mother-in-law? I wanted to be there for her, to be a helpful part of the family. But once again I was far away, as I had been on the day that Umma died.

That morning, she had become lucid for the first time in months and complained about her pain. Eun-Mi and Myoung-Hee took her to the hospital immediately, where she died within minutes of arrival.

It seemed an injustice that she would die in the same hospital as my father, whose death by drug overdose had preceded her death by only a year and a half. It was ironic that she had spent twenty years running away from him, only to be haunted by his memory in her illness and to die in the same place, her body sent to the same morgue.

More than anything, I wanted to be near Eun-Mi. I was alone in my grief, reduced to waterworks without warning while driving, dragging myself through the pointless monotony of employment, hugging my knees to my chest at night over a woman who was so far away that she sometimes seemed like a figment of my imagination. Carol claimed to be unaffected; she was busy with her own life and had only known Umma in a time so long ago that she couldn't remember. The two visits she had made in her adult life were not pleasant for her; she felt even more foreign than I. But I had felt a part of my family, and I wanted to be with my sisters the day they went to choose the headstone, the day they gathered for the funeral, during the long months of mourning that were to follow, and on New Year's Day and other holidays that they tended her grave.

My single day of bereavement leave was not going to help, and even if I could take off work on another unpaid leave, as I had in the spring, I didn't have enough money to pay for airfare. So I decided to have a memorial service for Umma in Minneapolis.

I scheduled the service for a Saturday so Mom and Dad would be able to come. I had thought about not telling them at all, because I didn't want to be hurt when they wouldn't come. But then optimism got the best of me, and I decided to invite them, anyway. I thought maybe the service would help them understand, and our family would be healed.

I telephone Mom the Saturday before.

"It would mean a lot if you would come." She makes some excuses, she'll have to think about it, Wal-Mart has a sale that day, she's planning a shopping trip to Fargo. "Mom, please come. I want you to come. It would mean so much to me."

She says she's *not interested*.

Each breath I take is very deep, from the belly. I have learned how to be in this family. I have learned how to live on the surface, how to say pleasing things so I will not make the smallest ripple, how to hold my voice and my face so that everything will remain unchanged. It's safe that way.

She is chatty today, planning her shopping trip, browsing the newspaper circulars, writing her list of mouthwash, deodorant, plastic storage containers. She is unaffected by my mother's death; it didn't happen, *she* didn't happen. In my mom's mind, I don't come from somewhere else, I don't have a birth mother, I don't, I don't.

I take another deep breath and weigh my choices. I can continue the charade or I can be true to myself. I opt for the latter. I'll say it. I'll name this illusion, this intractable lie.

She's still talking about Rubbermaid when I cut her off. "Can't you fucking come for the woman who gave you your children?" My voice is forcibly quiet. My chest tightens.

"*Say.*" She snaps it like a whip across my face. I can hear her hairline recede another inch and two more gray hairs sprout. I can feel her jaw tighten and her molars chipping right—over—the—phone. By now she is scribbling madly on her shopping list, pressing that twelve-for-eighty-nine-cents Bic as hard as she can, tracing over the same spiral patterns, over and over in infinite loops.

She has done it again. She can cow me into submission with a single word. I politely tell her, voice shaking, that I will not talk to her for a while. Good-bye.

I beep the phone off.

Sometimes I feel like a motherless child
A long way from home.
[TRADITIONAL SPIRITUAL]

Beauty tip: If you put spoons in the freezer for a few minutes and then place them over your eyes, the swelling will go down and no one will be able to tell that you've been crying all last night.

Mom can't understand why I'm on my high horse. Am I not the same daughter she raised, the one who mastered the methods of school, who always did her homework, who never made excuses, who practiced the piano without being told? If you raise your kids right, they shouldn't turn out . . . like . . . *this*. Did she not raise me to clean the house, weed the garden, master home economics? Did I not learn her rules? "Don't put it down; put it away. If you don't have time to do it now, when will you have time to do it? Do it right the first time." The Ten Commandments.

Loss is more than sadness.

Monday morning and I'm in my bathrobe, barefoot, smoking in the kitchen. I don't smoke. I dial up the people who are "for changing lives," Lutheran Social Service. Change *this*, I want to tell them. Give me information, every document you've collected about me and my parents, show me that in 1972 there was absolutely no information about what to do with a transracially adopted child, and that there is still no information available to them in their area, that you never gave them any support or follow-up. If their ignorance was beyond their control, maybe I could forgive their callous actions.

The receptionist answers with a cheery hello.

"Hello," I say in what I hope to be an equally cheery voice. I've learned how to approximate nice so I will get my way. "I was adopted through your agency in 1972. Who can I talk to so I can find out what my parents were told when they got me, or how they were screened?"

The voice on the other end of the line is blonde, fake effervescent, Lutheran. Doesn't have a clue or a care.

"I can refer you to Ms. X in our post-adoption services. One moment while I put you through to her."

Just my luck. Voice-mail.

"Hello, this is Ms. X. I'm not available to speak with you right now, but your call is important to me. Please leave your name and number, and I'll call you back as soon as I can." Beep.

"Hello, Ms. X. This is Jane Brauer. The front desk referred me to you. They said you might be able to talk with me about my adoption in 1972. Please call me at 612-364-0673. Thank you."

Tuesday morning and I'm in my bathrobe and I've just had a shot of Scotch when the phone rings.

"Hello, is this Jane? This is Ms. X from the adoption agency."

"Yes, thank you for calling me back. I'm, well, I'm having some problems, um, I was wondering if you can tell me who was the social worker who placed me with my parents in 1972, and if that person might still be available for me to talk with?" It was a stupid request; I couldn't think where to start.

"Oh, I don't think that person would still be here."

I light a cigarette and take a long drag.

"Okay, I understand that was a long time ago. Well, can you tell me if there are any support services for adult adoptees that I can use, or if I might be able to find out what my parents were told when they adopted me?"

"Well, I don't think I can help you with that. You should talk to Ms. Y for that information."

"All right. May I have her number please?"

I hang up and immediately dial the next number.

"Hello, Ms. Y. My name is Jane Brauer, and the agency referred me to Ms. X, who referred me to you to ask you some questions about my adoption in 1972. Do you have a moment?"

"Yes, how can I help you?"

"Well, I am having some problems with my family right now, and I'd really like to talk with the social worker who put my adoption through, or if that person is not working, I'd just like to find out what support services are available for adult adoptees. I also want to find out what my parents were told about international adoption before they got me."

"What year were you adopted?"

"1972."

"Oh, I don't think the social worker who placed you would work here any longer."

"Okay, I understand. Is it possible to find out what information my parents were given about international adoption?"

"I don't think they would have been given much information."

"Is it possible to open the file?"

"I'll have to do some looking. May I have Ms. Z call you back?"

"Sure. My number is 612-364-0673. May I have her number as well, just in case?"

"Please hold on. Ms. Z's number is 612-100-2000."

"Thank you. I look forward to hearing from her."

I let the cigarette butt burn in a dirty soup bowl. I dial the next number and conjure up my very best nonthreatening, cooperative, nice voice.

"Hello Ms. Z. I talked with Ms. Y concerning opening my adoption file from 1972. I was just wondering if you got the message. My name is Jane Brauer. I was adopted in November of 1972. Would you please call me back at 612-364-0673? Thank you.

Wednesday . . .

"Hello?"

"Hello. This is Ms. Z from LSS. Is Jane Brauer available?"

"Yes, this is Jane." I put on my Miss Congeniality voice. "Thank you for calling. I was wondering if I might be able to have some information about my adoption in 1972."

"Why do you need that?" The voice sounds irritated.

"Well, my birth mother has just died, and I'm having some problems with my adoptive family. I would like to find out what they were told about international adoption when they got me."

"Can't you talk to your parents about it?"

"No, we're ... we're not speaking. Is it possible to see my file or get a copy of it?"

"What are your parents' names?"

"Frederick and Margaret Brauer."

"If you can hold, I'll put you through to our assistant, Ms. A."

"Thank you." Click.

"Hello, Jane?"

"Yes, this is Jane."

"This is Ms. A. I have your file right here." The voice is young and casual. She must be a college intern. She's probably writing a paper about adoption. I could tell her a thing or two that she won't learn at the agency.

"Great! Is it possible for me to come in to see it, or may I get a copy?"

"No, I'm afraid you can't do that."

"Well, you're looking at it right now, aren't you?" I have obviously interrupted her nail-filing itinerary for today.

"Yes, but you can't have access to this information."

"Well, can you tell me what's in it? Can you tell me about the home study or the social worker who conducted it? Can you tell me what classes or information your agency provided for my parents?" I try to control my voice, which careens between shouting and crying.

"No, I'm sorry, we're not able to give that information out."

"Oh."

"Can I help you with anything else?"

I swallow hard and take a breath. Don't cry on the phone. Don't scream at her just because she, a perfect stranger with probably minimal qualifications, can sit there and read my file with all my information in it and all my family's information and all the crap that determined my life and *I am not allowed*. Don't ask her to bend the policy just this one time, because she could get into trouble. This happened a long time before she got involved.

"Well, I was wondering if there are any support groups or something for adult adoptees? I'm having a hard time with my adoptive family. I noticed that most of the groups are for either adoptive parents or younger adoptees, like age ten."

"I don't know of any, but you should call Ms. B. She might know. You could also call Ms. C, Ms. D, or Ms. E. Here are their numbers."

"Hello Ms. B, I just talked with LSS, and they said you might know something about support groups for adult adoptees?"

"I know there are some people interested in starting one, but I don't know if there's anything yet. You should call Ms. A at . . ."

"She's the person who referred me to you."

"Oh. You could also talk with Ms. X, or Ms. E. Their numbers are . . ."

"Thanks, Ms. A gave me those numbers. I'll call them. Thanks."

"Hello Ms. C, I'm looking for a support group for adult adoptees, and Ms. A referred me to you. Do you know of anything available for people in the Twin Cities?"

"I think that Ms. D has something. You should also try Ms. B. If you hold, I'll transfer you to my colleague here, and she can give you those phone numbers."

"That's all right, I already have them. Thank you."

"Hello Ms. D. My name is Jane Brauer . . ."

"I heard Ms. C . . ."

Etc.

I finally talk with someone helpful, who tells me to call Heather at Lutheran Social Service. I'm instructed to call her post-adoption secretary, then give the secret password: "personal call." I dial up the secretary and give the password, and, amazingly, I am transferred immediately to Heather, who is at her desk the moment I call. She tells me that she is a Korean adoptee herself, which is *my* secret password: I know I can trust this woman.

She tells me that I should come in and talk with her, no charge. Just come in and see what needs to be done.

The address is in south Minneapolis, an area populated by run-down mansions, exchanged for new suburban homes by their owners in the seventies, when the fuel prices went through the roof and the owners couldn't afford to heat the huge houses in the bite of Minnesota winter. Lutheran Social Service is in a flat, brick building, decidedly late-sixties. I enter the building with a sense of foreboding; I have never been here, but here is where my life in America began.

I arrive in the waiting room fifteen minutes early for my ten o'clock appointment with Heather. I introduce myself to the secretary, with whom I must have spoken on the phone. Probably the one who read my file as just a normal part of her workday, the one who wouldn't tell me what was inside my own file. Sure enough, she is young, blonde, a cheerful do-gooder. I'm sure she's the offspring of some matronly woman who wears appliqués on her sweatshirts, the one known for her excellent tuna casseroles at church potlucks.

I leaf through the magazines on the side table in the waiting room. They are filled with pictures of orphans waiting to be adopted from Romania and China—cute, happy children guaranteed to fall in love with their new parents instantly. One success story (aren't they all success stories?) shows a photograph of a beaming brown-haired boy, eager as a squirrel, wearing a T-shirt with an American flag emblazoned across the chest.

> George's birth mother abandoned him at a dormitory in Romania. He lived there three years with sixteen roommates, living on only soup and bread. When Bob and Marilyn adopted him about two years ago, he quickly blossomed in his forever family. "He's absolutely the happiest child I have ever met in my life," said George's father. "He's totally 'Mr. Happy.' He's always smiling. When people meet him for the first time, they always ask, 'Doesn't he ever have a bad day?'"

Other pictures show happy "motherland" tour groups posing in front of tourist traps and adopted Korean girls dressed in hanboks, happy as pie and obviously American. That shameless American smile gives them away, and the way they make their hanboks look gaudy instead of elegant. Everybody is so fucking happy.

Heather rushes into the waiting room at exactly ten o'clock, wearing a sweater and loose black-and-white-checkered slacks. I recognize her instantly although I've never met her before; the secret identification code—*I'm adopted Korean*—also means "Look for a Korean wearing comfortable clothes."

She seats me in her office, and I'm surprised at my own mental disconnect: here is a Korean face speaking to me in perfectly good English, and a Minnesota accent to boot. Her eyebrows impress me. Asian eyebrows tend to grow downward, and she's mastered whatever trick it is that gets them to look like they're growing upward in perfect arches. She has the kind of eyelids that fold in on themselves; a carefully placed line of black eyeliner makes her large brown eyes seem even larger. She wears coral lipstick, the glossy kind. A large diamond engagement ring and wedding band adorn her perfect manicure.

I like her. She reminds me of Carol.

She tells me about herself, about when she was adopted in that first wave from the Holt Agency, about how she's friends with an adopted Korean moviemaker—did I see her movie on PBS?—and about her kids, whose photographs adorn her otherwise sterile social worker's office.

I wonder how often she gets put in this situation, how often Lutheran Social Service deflects pissed-off adoptees into her office, where they are immediately disarmed by her charm and understanding. Whatever, it works. She puts me at ease, turns the faceless adoption bureaucracy into a mom-and-pop shop run by some half-Korean kid's friendly mom. She seems to have this all figured out, both for herself and for everyone else.

I trust her and like her so much that I dismiss my regular good manners and polite vocabulary, reminding myself that this is her job, after all, and explode into a hyperventilating, shaking mess.

She listens carefully, and she understands. How absolutely amazing. She comments, "It sounds like your dad is a more feeling person. You should try to talk with him alone and see if he'll come to the memorial service." She notes that it is bothersome that my parents sound like they're "invested in being ignorant." Best of all, she gives me permission to not talk with my parents except on my own terms.

～

My dad has worked at the same sheet metal factory for more than thirty years. In that time, I've called him at work once. It was an emergency.

He's a riveter, not an office worker, so he doesn't have his own phone, and I know that talking to him means he'll be standing in a semi-public place, only after I've gone through a secretary, waited until his break, called back at a precise ten-minute interval, then had him paged. But Heather has suggested this, and, being optimistic and still hoping for something healing to happen, I think, *Why not try.*

I don't spend much time with small talk. Dad doesn't have a long break.

"Please come to the memorial service, even if Mom doesn't. Do you remember how sad you were when your mom died? I feel like that now. That's why I would like you to come."

Silence.

"Dad?"

"You swore at my wife. We're not coming."

In a family that doesn't talk much, the value of each word rises. There is no chitchat or further explanation, no second chances, and no "I feel _____ when _____ because _____ " statements. You learn to decipher the true meaning from a few clues, through echolocation, the way a bat bounces a sound wave off here and there, so it can navigate, despite blindness, by a signal that cuts through empty space. You learn to extract from two sparse sentences that your mom and dad are producing their united front, and that acknowledging your loss would mean acknowledging that there was something there in the first place, something worth having. They do not understand that you have love enough for them and your Korean family because they have love only for you. You learn that they cannot understand why you have a need to express your feelings about your Umma's death because they never expressed their feelings when their own parents died. They feel betrayed. They're taking a side against you because they feel you're taking a side against them, siding with those Koreans. You are no longer their daughter. You are not wanted.

> *My life goes on in endless song*
> *above earth's lamentations.*
> *I hear the sweet though far-off hymn*
> *that hails a new creation.*
>
> [ROBERT LOWRY]

The morning of the memorial service, Father Michael called, asking if I still wanted to go through with it. At least a foot of snow had fallen the night before, and the sound of plows and snow blowers echoed through the quiet Minneapolis neighborhood. Christmas was approaching and Mark and I planned to leave soon for New York, so I said yes.

Father Michael had asked me to bring photographs of my mother since there was no body. I brought one photograph in a pine frame with some candles and her letters to me, tied up in a bundle, and set them on a table at the front of the church. It was a small display, nothing like the kind you see at graduations and anniversary parties, with huge pieces of tag board covered in photographs spanning twenty or thirty years. I had spent a total of seven weeks with Umma that I could remember. For four of those seven weeks, she was ill. I had one picture of her alone in good health, and this was the one I brought.

The memorial service was a small affair. I had invited only my closest friends, people who understand that funerals are for the living, not the dead. The one person attending who had actually met my mother, besides me, was Mrs. Han.

Mrs. Han had translated for Umma and me five years earlier, the day that we were reunited. "That little woman," she says, shaking her head as she looks at the photo display, knowing Umma's story and her hard life. Umma smiles out at her from the photograph. Mrs. Han and Umma both lived through the Japanese occupation of Korea; they are contemporaries, both having witnessed the division of a nation and the loss of its children.

"*Kamsahamnida*. Thank you for coming. My mother would have appreciated this," I say to her. It is so good to see her Korean face on this day. I hadn't talked with Mrs. Han for five years, not since the tour, but when I called her and left the message, stammering, "I don't know if you remember me," she was able to sort through all my awkwardness and uncertain words; she remembered me, and she remembered my family, as my family. Here she is, on this snowy, cold day.

Oksana walks into the little church with snow on her shoulders. "Jane!" she exclaims in her beautiful Russian accent. She understands what it is to have family far away; for ten years she has lived apart from her mother and sister in Moscow. She and her husband and children sit behind Janet, who has somehow managed to release herself from her three young children for something she regards as important.

At the front of the church, Dick examines the photographs. I have asked him to come as a proxy for my own parents, since he has two adopted Korean children, who are elementary school–aged. He reverently folds his hands together while he looks into the face of my mother, the same way people pay respect to the body of the deceased. I admire his bravery; he doesn't talk about Peter and Leah's birth families with them, but he has found the courage to honor mine. I can see that behind his red beard, he is wondering when this will happen in his family.

LaGretta seats herself in a pew at the back. We exchange knowing looks. She's a woman of tremendous power, the kind of power that can only be earned. She doesn't mince words, but she is always gracious. She loves children. She has raised two of her own into balanced, happy young adults, and I respect her enormously.

Father Michael reads Bible passages that are meant to be comforting. I desperately want to believe these words about life after death and resurrection and eternal glory, but I don't.

He calls me up to read. I have chosen a letter from Umma, to give her a voice on this last day. I begin: "Dear my daughters Mi-Ja and Kyong-Ah! . . ."

After two paragraphs, my breath comes in choppy, violent gasps. I cannot speak. Mark saves me; he approaches the pulpit, touches my hand as he takes the letter, and finishes reading for me.

My friends all hug me as they leave. I cry in front of people who have never seen me cry before, people to whom I am always polite and cheery. Now they see me without the smile. I leave wet spots on their wool coats. They speak to me quietly and gently. Sympathy cards gather on a pew.

> *Through all the tumult and the strife*
> *I hear the music ringing,*
> *It finds an echo in my soul.*
> *How can I keep from singing?*
> [ROBERT LOWRY]

It was a quiet kind of mourning. A deep, stillborn loss.

Not long after Christmas, Mark's grandmother died of cancer. Seeing her in the hospital was hard; I knew this face of sickness too well. I sent his mother the kind of care package that I would have liked to give myself when Umma died: fancy soaps, chocolates, comforting things for the senses.

I quit my job—my first "real" job out of college. It was a full-time, nonprofit job, directing a music school I had designed to give music lessons for "families who could not otherwise afford quality instruction." But I had nothing left to give, no desire to help others. After I heard the umpteenth sad story about how such and such family was so poor that they couldn't continue to buy Internet access/cable TV/ soccer uniforms, I found someone to take my place and walked.

Being spiritually bankrupt, I thought maybe I should just make obscene amounts of money. So I started school for computer programming. But within a couple of months, I quit that, too.

I dropped out of everything.

> To be explicit, no Caucasian children from any
> country are being referred to us for placement in the
> United States . . . Practically speaking, we can only
> suggest Korean children—both pure Korean and Korean-
> Caucasian or Korean-Negro—for interested families.
>
> [INTERNATIONAL SOCIAL SERVICE, 1970]

Highly prized, American-born, healthy Caucasian infants were still readily available for adoption in the late 1950s. My friend Mary was one of them.

Her emerald-cut diamond, set in a wide gold band, reflects the light from the street, throwing geometric patterns of rainbow colors onto the table. Her second husband must love her very much to have given her a ring like that, and what's not to love? Her wavy blonde hair reaches the middle of her back, her earnest blue eyes are almost too large for her slim face, and she always polishes her nails in a bright metallic color. She rides an Oldenburg gelding, which I'm sure is the physical representation of her true spirit—powerful, graceful, and willful, with a long black mane and tail reminiscent of Black Beauty and all the other horses in storybooks girls love.

Mary and I talk about being "people-pleasers," about how children can misunderstand all the parental hoopla about being "chosen," thinking it means they can also be "unchosen." We talk about how romantic relationships can be destructive, developing much too quickly before we realize that we are not very attached to this man at all, and about how friendships come and go if we don't work at them.

I tell her that I've been feeling depressed since my mother died. "I don't have the energy to move. I just want to lie in bed all day, and then if I happen to muster up the energy to go somewhere, I'll start bawling in the grocery store, or the gas station, or wherever."

"Well, you know what they say. All depression is anger turned in on yourself, and all anger is about injustice."

Then she lays another one on me that I haven't thought about: "Your parents will always hate you on some level because you are not who you are supposed to be."

She says it as if she has known it a long time, and although she is a mother of a teenager herself, the hurt of the little girl is still there.

Hate me?

It is true that my parents wanted white boys. They wanted to name them Robert and Charles, and what they got was a nephew named Robert, a mean barn cat named Charlie, and two Korean girls with strange names that had to be changed.

Mary and I are replacement children. We are children who were not adopted because there was "room for one more" or, as is the case more rarely, the adoptive parents only wanted adopted children because they felt it was the right thing to do. Mary and I are last resorts; consolation prizes in the fertility lottery; the children who came into the family to replace the biological child, the child who was really wanted.

Of course, none of this is verbalized. But children, keenly sensitive to the unspoken world, feel it. We didn't know that we could never be good enough, so we kept trying to do the impossible. We were like pathetic little dogs. *Oh, please, love me, pet me, tell me what to do so I can do it for you. Shall I sit? Shall I stay? How long? Do you like me?*

Mary's words hit home. I had never thought that my own parents hated me. But maybe there is some truth to that. To our parents, we are reminders of their infertility. We are reminders that something is wrong with someone's body, with someone's womanhood or someone's manhood. We are reminders of inadequacy, of incompleteness. Of course, nobody on the outside thinks that, but shame carries its own version of the truth.

Mary continues, her ring glinting in the sun. "It doesn't matter how good in school you are, or how clean you keep your house, or what a good mother you are. You can never be good enough for your parents. You will always have that strange feeling you can't shake even though you corner them and demand to know what they want from you. What they want from you is for you to be someone you're not. They'll never say to your face, 'You are not the child we wanted. You were second choice, second best.' But that's the truth. Underneath all the 'adoption is wonderful' rhetoric, the truth is there and they're ashamed to even acknowledge it themselves. They will never say it, but you know it. Because you always have that nagging feeling that you're not good enough."

I guess I never made any plans for myself. I never made it to grad school, never set a specific career goal. In college, I merely checked off requirements, setting one foot in front of the other. After that I accepted whatever fell into my lap, from the Deaf Relay job to the music school. Maybe that was the PTSD manifesting, or maybe it was laziness and apathy.

Despite being an intellectual slob, I somehow ended up having exceedingly smart friends who read exceedingly smart books and helped me make connections between tasty snacks and authors like Proust.

When I started dating Mark, I wanted to impress him using Mom's love-through-feeding technique, so I checked out a library book on Vietnamese cooking (Vietnamese, Korean—white guy didn't really know the difference) and prepared exotic dinners designed to make him feel lucky, as in Lucky Money, Lucky Bamboo, Lucky Dragon, Lucky You Got an Asian Girlfriend.

A bonus feature of Vietnamese cooking is that it contains a good deal of French influence due to the occupation. I tried the recipe for orange madeleines: delicious! The obsession was born.

A long list of experiments took place in the following months: clementine madeleines, corn and country ham madeleines, Grand Marnier madeleines, Absolut Citron madeleines. I finally found the perfect recipe: Julia Child's lemony Proustian madeleines, with more butter and less flour than I thought possible, and oh-so-delicious with their little humped backs, created by boiling the butter before adding it to the batter. A dusting of powdered sugar shook through a tea strainer completes them.

After the memorial service, I needed something to lift my spirits. Preferably something not having anything to do with reality.

I decided to throw a "Proust Party" and invited all my literati friends for a pretentious afternoon of lavender tea and assorted madeleines, plus Proust imitations, hoping someone would volunteer to lie in my bed and shiver. I asked everyone to bring a teacup to swap as well as a book by Proust or another writer equally as effete. I had already read Alain de Botton's *How Proust Can Change Your Life* and was ready to tackle *Remembrance of Things Past*, the whole thing, with just two weeks to go until the big bash.

I went to the public library and requested the book in the newest translation possible, one from the mid-eighties. A week later, it arrived. The librarian pulled it from behind the counter, a sad blue hardback without a dust cover, a big stain on the front, strings hanging out of the spine. I asked the librarian to double-check to make sure it was the right book. Indeed, it was, this book that looked at least fifty years older than the one I requested. So I checked it out, walked home, and decided that now, with one week before the Proust party, I had better start reading.

I spent an hour reading Proust's description of lying in bed. That was Chapter One. I started Chapter Two. Then I skimmed the index. Then something unexpected fell out of the book, a quarter sheet of paper—

PRIVILEGE REQUEST

Name of Client _____

Privileges Requested _____

Specify Length of Time and

    Any Conditions _____

Reason for Request _____

Signed (Counselor) _____

Another piece of paper was tucked inside the same pages, a small notebook sheet with almost illegible writing, words crossed out and replaced. The top of this sheet was filled with scribbles, where the author tried to coax the ink from his pen. Finally, the words came out:

Any autobiography that I might attempt to present without the excision of most sordid details and a mythically and optically distorted social perspective would undermine the fairly uncommon life which I have led. I am willing to attempt to present the salient myths and matters of "pinned down" historical fact which have dominated the picture as I have lurched and bounded through life.

A palm reader on Fillmore Street (in S.F.) once told me that my paws prognosed a very long life, but one over which I would have very little control. That diagnosis has held up well. I have survived 41 years of age—still alive even often against my own will and provocation.

I was surely the black sheep of a white middle class small Minnesota Irish Catholic country family. We lived on a small horse farm, seven miles out of town. My father was gone often in my early years as the district manager of a grocery chain and later was home when he had purchased his own grocery store.

These facts are insignificant.

Several things seem important to my current social disposition. First, I was raised with little prejudice regarding any minorities, either economic or racial, since my community was pretty homogenous. My sexual role models were nearly entirely the reverse of societal norms—my mother was strong physically and psychologically dominating, not too verbal or creative, my father embodied characteristics of manipulativeness, nurturing, gentleness, and submissiveness and verbalness, which were at that time attributed to women.

My sense of who I was with regard to much the world was ambiguous.

I didn't finish the Proust, but the party was a success, and all the madeleines eaten.

I had been thinking about writing for a while. It was an old habit, a palimpsest from the days when I was compelled to do it and other people were compelled to read the results and interrogate me. Diaries were dangerous. I learned that lesson many times, first with my mom and then with jealous boyfriends, until the compulsion to write was finally buried. I had concluded that writing, even if only for myself, was out of the question.

Then this piece of paper, a kind of message in a bottle from a stranger capsized in a mental hospital, came all wrapped up in *Remembrance of Things Past*. I couldn't help but take it as a sign. I began to write.

> I am Jane Marie Brauer, created September 26, 1972, when I was carried off an airplane onto American soil . . .

Never lacking the ability to second-guess myself, I decide that maybe I was a little bit hysterical the last time I called Lutheran Social Service, and with the benefit of almost a year to let my temper cool, I decide to try again. Maybe I'll be able to control my emotions better this time; maybe I'll get someone who wants to help me.

The question is still the same: May I see my file?

With the cool, friendly voice of someone who wants something, I call Adoption, am transferred to Post-Adoption, talk to a gum-snapping young woman who asks me to send her an e-mail. I send the e-mail, get no response, call again. The next week I get the same gum-snapper who doesn't remember ever talking to me. I ask to talk with her supervisor.

The supervisor has a nasal, reedy voice. She operates under the same assumptions as everyone else, it appears, and doesn't question the myths. I intend to ask her the hard questions.

Q: May I see my file?

A: No. There's a law against that. That's your parents' privacy.

Q: Okay. I know how to use the law library. May I have the name of that law so I may read it for myself?

A: I'm sorry, I don't know what that is.

Q: Is it really a law or is it just a policy of LSS?

A: That's our policy.

Q: Do you have a written statement of your policies that is available for people to see?

A: No.

Q: Does my file still exist?

A: Yes.

Q: Where is it kept?

A: It's here.

Q: Is it in your building on Park Avenue?

A: Yes.

Q: If I can't see it, what do you use it for?

A: We don't use it, but by law, we have to keep it.

Q: Do you know the name of that law?

A: No.

Q: Is this also a real law, or is it a policy?

A: I don't know.

Q: Who would I talk to in order to get the policy changed?

A: You can write a letter to me.

Q: I'm talking to you right now, so why do I need to write to you?

A:

Q: Okay, well, if it's not possible to see my file, I'm wondering if you have records of old advertisements about adopting through LSS, ones that my parents may have seen; I'm interested in learning how they found out about Korean adoption. Do you still have those?

A: No, we wouldn't have kept those.

Q: Were there any programs available to them before or after adoption?

A: Somebody mentioned a Korea program. The parents were invited to have a Korean meal.

Q: Were these programs mandatory?

A: I don't know.

I can't believe a supervisor would know so little about her job. I can see one of two possibilities: either she knows and she won't tell me, or she truly doesn't know and she ought not be working there.

She suggests a support group at Lutheran Social Service (if she would just fork over the damn information, I wouldn't need a support group) and tells me that for thirty-five dollars they will open my Korean placement file. The thing she doesn't understand is that I don't need my Korean placement file, and even if I did, why should I pay them thirty-five dollars to open a file and make a copy? Haven't they already made enough money off me?

The urge to commiserate led me to alter my unintentionally all-white world by actively seeking out other Asians. I found a few locals who had friends, and these friends had friends, and before long my e-mail address was added to every political Asian's list in the Twin Cities. Then the KKK came to town.

When it was time to stand on the capitol steps and protest the KKK as a group, I offended people with my absence and my defense of my absence: I couldn't see how protesting as an insular racial group was supposed to help end racism; giving the KKK media attention was exactly what they wanted, anyway; my ideas about volunteering in schools as a means of change and education were apparently too naïve or mainstream or something.

Despite my requests to be taken off the lists, my in-box was flooded with everybody's Pan-Asian opinion about everything, including myself in third person: "Who is SHE and how does she IDENTIFY anyway?" they asked incredulously. It was as if I had forgotten to flash my *Überasiangemeinschaft* ID card to the bouncer at the Asians-only power club.

I confused the Überasians because I didn't fit neatly into their group. I wuzn't dissin' white people; I didn't have the correct assumptions and conspiracy theories. Insulting white men for dating yellow women or yellow women for dating white men only made me defensive about my relationship with Mark. I didn't nurse a deep hatred of America and all the white people in it. Mostly I wondered if, had these Überasians been white and the target of their racist comments black, or vice versa, the FBI would have a file on them.

There were some other adopted Koreans lurking around in that group—I knew because they privately sent me very sweet and supportive e-mails—but they must have already learned that showing one's creamy white banana-flavored center would be enough to get exiled from the pack. They knew you could be reviled for marrying interracially, for living and working in a white environment, for not having enough Asian Pride.

For weeks following the big e-mail blowout, I stewed in self-loathing. I caught myself having shameful thoughts: *If they don't like it here, why don't they go back to where they came from?* It was as if those childhood taunts from Harlow came back to rest in my own mouth. But mostly I loathed myself because—once again, what a big surprise—I wasn't accepted. Still not Asian enough, suspected of being a subcutaneous white supremacist. Was all my time spent in Korea for nothing? Would I have to not only learn to be Korean but also to shoulder the responsibility of being Pan-Asian-Pacific-Islander-political-activist-representative-for-most-of-the-world? After all my time with my family, was I still a fraud, a grotesque hybrid?

What to Do with Memories

Spread them out across the table. Build a fence to keep some out and others in. Build a tower so high and delicate that the ancestors must answer prayers. Build a small, square house of interlocking words to shelter the unborn, to keep them from the things that frighten and maim. Boil a soup and feed it to the body politic which has given its stones to children to carry. Feed it to those who do not wish to taste both sweet and bitter from the same bowl, whose stomachs are full of feathery illusions, whose eyes do not see that children are tricksters who serve gratitude and shame, who fool adults as easily as greed and desire.

Through the benevolence of an archival university librarian who still harbored the apparently defunct idea that information should be available and free, I was able to contact a sociology professor with connections. She in turn allowed me to use her name in order to request an appointment with the president and CEO of LSS. If I couldn't get any answers from the bottom up, I'd take the top down.

Sure enough, I dropped the magic, university-level name and called myself a researcher—not an adoptee—and I had an appointment scheduled in less than a minute.

By this time, I had accepted the fact that I did not have the right to read the American file pertaining to my adoption. I would settle for general information about LSS's practices at the time.

I made sure I got there early. I sat in the parking lot in my car, making a list of questions that I would ask Mr. CEO:

1. Was there advertising for Korean adoption in rural Minnesota in the 1970s? What was the nature of the advertising?
2. What kind of training was provided for the adoption social workers who placed children?
3. What kind of information did LSS provide adoptive parents about international/interracial adoption?
4. Were there mandatory classes for prospective parents?

5. What kind of follow-up took place in adoptive families?
6. How are LSS records used?
7. What is the logic of having a law that they must be kept if they're not accessible to those who need them?

As the professor had warned me, Mr. CEO didn't have all the answers. But I didn't feel angry with him because I didn't get the sense that he was trying to get rid of me or that I was inconveniencing him.

In fact, he spent over an hour with me, just talking about general stuff, not really answering my questions, but not because he didn't want to. He just didn't know. It was a good discussion. He offered me coffee; he looked comfortable in his corner office with his clean shoes. His job was concerned with the larger picture of LSS, of which international adoption is only a very small part. LSS does most of its work with financial and debt counseling.

Similar to Heather the counselor, with whom I'd met nearly a year before that, what made Mr. CEO so wonderful was not that he had all the answers. He had very few, if any. But he listened to me as if he were truly interested in how this grand experiment had turned out. He understood that behind all those names and case numbers were real children, and one of them was me, and that I had come to see him personally. He saw my humanity, my value as a person, not just a case file in a program that was closed years ago.

In order to find some general information pertaining to international adoption in the 1970s, Mr. CEO introduced me to his Director of Communications, Mr. BS. Mr. CEO reiterated my request for general information—old pamphlets and so forth—and extracted an affirmative answer from Mr. BS that these things were probably in the basement and could be found. Mr. BS gave me his business card, wrote down my personal information, and promised to get back to me.

He didn't. I called and e-mailed him over the ensuing months, reminding him of our conversation; he replied that he had been too busy with other things.

The reporting is the vengeance—not the beheading, not the gutting, but the words. And I have so many words— "chink" words and "gook" words too—that they do not fit on my skin.

[MAXINE HONG KINGSTON, THE WOMAN WARRIOR]

When you're coming out of the closet, it helps to have friends with experience.

Aaron is a tenor, but he can crank it up to countertenor; he plays "Caesar," a cross-dressing vocal coach, in a local cabaret show; his roommate is a beauty pageant–winning drag queen; and, oh yes, he's from Big Fork, Minnesota.

We're perched cross-legged on stools at T.G.I. Friday's after a musical rehearsal; in a week we'll perform a selection of songs from RuPaul, Bette, and Barbra. He wears a turtleneck, corduroys, and turquoise suede Hush Puppies; he holds a glass of red wine in one hand while smoking a cigarette he bummed from a cute waiter with the other.

I met Aaron when I was a senior in college and he was an incoming freshman. He was moody for awhile—awkward, slightly overweight, unsure of whether he wanted to play piano or clarinet, to sing, compose, or conduct, or to just become an English major. So he did all of it. Then he came out and became downright depressed. Then he became fabulous.

I've come to Aaron for comfort because we have so much in common, meaning we're both from the hinterlands of rural Minnesota; our parents are both overly Lutheran (his dad is a pastor); we both have characteristics that would be easier to live without. Meaning he's gay and I'm Korean. Born like that. No choice.

"Were your mom and dad really mad when you told them you were gay?"

"Are you kidding? Of course! They completely cut me off, wouldn't help me with college, nothing. But now we're on speaking terms again, if you can call it that. I just don't let it bother me when my mom leaves right-wing Christian pamphlets in my backpack. Dr. James Dobson thinks he has the answer for everything."

"I remember him. My mom read all his books. So, did they kind of suspect that you were gay all along?"

"They might have thought about it, but really, that's the last thing they could possibly want in their lives."

"Yeah, that's like my mom and dad. They suspected I might be Korean, but they were hoping it wasn't true."

This business about identity must be serious. As much as I'd like to yawn it off and relegate it to the obsessions of teenagers, trying out this hair style and these clothes and this extracurricular activity until they find one they really like, I know that announcing "Mom, Dad, I'm K-K-Korean. No, you don't get it, I mean, I'm *Korean*," is a lot more difficult than deciding to become a pianist. And after I acknowledge that I'm Korean—or at least an adopted one—like Aaron, I am not going to magically "move on" or become "normal."

"Was there a time that you didn't talk to your parents at all?" I ask Aaron.

"Oh, I didn't talk to them for a couple of years," he says breezily, part of his gay man persona. "But when I finally did," and now he grows truly serious, "I said, do you think I'd be gay if I had a *choice?*" He raises his voice. "Do you know how fucking hard it is to be gay in this family? Do you think I *want* this?"

Aaron may as well be adopted. When I came with him to visit his family, I couldn't believe how someone who looked so much like everyone else could also look so different. His mannerisms, speech, everything—he could have been from outer space.

He tried to fit into his hometown for years: he played football, shot deer, tried to date girls. A few hundred landmines later, he's gay with a vengeance, and I'm proud of him. He can still be moody, but on the whole he's happier because he's found a graceful way to be true to himself. By surrounding himself with friends who love him for who he is, he has built up an enormous emotional reservoir that allows him to give both to friends like me and to people who are not

friends, who need to be educated. He can do all this in high heels, fish-
net stockings, and fake eyelashes, all the while singing and dancing in
his own genuine, irrepressible, super way.

My dear Umma,

Now that you are dead, you are more near to me. You've always
been so far away, halfway across the earth in your basement apartment
in Seoul, me here in Minnesota trying so hard to learn your language
and failing, calling you just to hear your voice but understanding only
one phrase: "*Saranghayo*. I love you." But now, I talk to you all the time.
I talk to you in English, and I think I hear you talking to me in English,
or emotions, or maybe it is something else, but I can understand it. I
have dreams now. They are in Korean, and they must be from you.
Because now I can read, Umma, I can really read in Korean, and I thank
you for somehow giving me this. It's magical, because I never could
read when you were alive.

Umma, do you see your picture that I have set out on the bureau
in my living room? It is the same one we used at your memorial service, the one I took five years ago, when we met each other for the first
time since you sent me to America. You are sitting on the floor, a mis-
chievous smile on your face, healthy, tanned from the bright Seoul
sun, wearing your set of casual clothes, pink flower pants, a beige knit
top. You are looking straight at me, at the camera. I peer closely into
the picture, searching for a detail that I haven't noticed before, anything new. I think if I look long enough I may be taken past the surface of the picture, through a portal into another world, or that I will
notice something moving in the picture, proving that you are still living, only in a different place. You continue to smile, to look straight
ahead. Do you see that I try to honor you by lighting candles and
incense, by leaving food out for you? I left new shoes for you, a map
of one of the mountains with the temple at the top, some money
that you might need for your journey. When I cook Korean food, I
hope you see how much I miss you, and that when I eat the kimchi,

the bulgogi, mandu, bibimbop, all of the things that I love, I am filled for a moment with a reminder of you and the things that were taken from me. I take you back, and I take back all the things that were stolen, back inside my body.

Your daughter,
Kyong-Ah

捌

Exile's Crossword

```
              K     M
          M O T H E R
              R     M
      J U X T A P O S E   M O
      A       M     A     O R
A   J A N U S   E         U R Y   M
M     E     F R A U D     M     B E
B           I             M     T   S
I           C       L A N G U A G E
V       P A R A D O X         M   E
A   B           E             O   M
L A U G H         N E I T H E R
E   T       S     I         E   P
N   T     K Y O N G A H     R   H
T   E       Z             M   O
  D R E A M Y         F R E A K S
    F       G   L         P   I
  A L C H E M Y   O     B O T H   S
    Y           S         R
          S U S P E N S I O N     S
                        D       T
                        I       O
          S U B L I M A T I O N E
                        E       E
```

Words appearing in the grid:

MOTHER
JUXTAPOSE
JANUS
FRAUD
LANGUAGE
PARADOX
LAUGH
NEITHER
KYONGAH
DREAM
FREAKS
ALCHEMY
BOTH
SUSPENSION
SUBLIMATION
AMBIVALENT
MEMORY
STONE

～

A simple question put me in search of a word to describe, to accurately nail down my existence. The question was this: "Would you rather have been raised in Korea?"

I looked into her blue eyes, this intelligent, third-generation American whom I truly like, then looked away and mumbled something about how it's impossible to say; I would have had different values if I had been raised in Korea; my sisters turned out fine, but you never know, etc.

In adoption there is a tension between seeming and being: between the shining outside—the happy smiles of adoptive parents, the expectations of happily ever after, the how-to-adopt books, the lovely picture books with no mention of a child's birth mother—and the reality of the heart.

If only I could find the courage to speak, to articulate what I know instead of nodding politely, changing the subject. If only I had the guts to challenge someone's assumptions. Would I rather have been raised in Korea?

For my friend, the question is rhetorical and the answer is clear. She's been told that I was "saved" and "born not under my mother's heart, but in it." I have been rescued by adoption; had I stayed in Korea, I would have been institutionalized, after which I would have turned into what Asian girls tend to turn into if left to their own devices: a prostitute. The standards by which she judges good living—a college education, American citizenship, a white, middle-class upbringing in a pre-approved home—would not have been available to me.

Newly adoptive parents close to my age like to comfort me. "Big people make choices for little people," they explain. Gently, as if I am the age of their toddlers, they work out the convenient and fateful equation for me: my parents didn't have children and I needed a home.

For me, it's not so simple. I wish that my adoption was a one-hundred-percent-positive thing, that people as well as God did not see the color of skin, that having grown to be the tallest of my siblings was a sign not only of good childhood nutrition but of spiritual abundance as well. How do I explain in the course of polite conversation that my seemingly flawless assimilation into America has yielded anything but joy and gratitude? How do I explain my ambivalence? Yet I do have mixed feelings. I feel ashamed and unworthy of the gifts that have been given me; ashamed for not being a better daughter—both a grateful American one and a forgiving Korean one, guided by filial piety; ashamed for opening my mouth, despite everything people have tried to do for me, in what they thought were my best interests. What an unworthy, spoiled, ungrateful, whining, American brat.

The way I think about myself these days is with the word that best describes me: exile. I hadn't thought of myself as an exile or immigrant before—just a lucky adoptee. But now, I see that "exile" is the word that fits me best.

The language of exile is filled with gains and losses, culture and family, memory and imagination. I try on the identity of exile, and it feels good. Not that it feels good to be an exile, but it feels good to have something fit. "Adoptee" never seemed quite right; it didn't address what I had lost, which was an inseparable part of what I had gained.

I have little patience for "ex-pates" who ricochet around the globe in search of the perfect café, willing women, cheap wine. Yet there are some whose experiences resonate with me; for those who find their place, their second home, yearning is transformed into something else, something ghostly yet real as flesh.

There is the absurdity of the exile poet who writes in his native language and none of his friends in his new country can read it. It's like the terrible absurdity I encounter when I cannot talk to my own family. There is the exile who visits the graves of his Jewish ancestors in Alexandria; he washes the stone lovingly, and I am reminded of my own wish to visit my mother's grave, to touch it and bow before the woman who gave birth to me, who watches over me now from far away. There is the feeling of displacement, of longing for there when you're here; of creating a world inside that is a substitute for the one outside, because the one inside can hold everything tightly in one place, unlike the vast world where so many beloved people and places are scattered beyond reach. There is the willing exile who lives in France, studying the language and blundering through, like me going into a Korean restaurant and saying to the waitress, "Thank you very much. Never mind. Are you full." There is the willing ex-pate who finds a home elsewhere, amongst her grandmother's people, and returns there every year to soak up the beauty of a beaten and glorious old city.

These things that other writers ruminate on—the feeling of home-sickness, the sense of being at home nowhere but comfortable in many places, the power of memory—are realities, yet luxuries of the intelligentsia.

Where is the outpouring of reflection from the Somali taxi driver in Minneapolis, the shopkeeper at Halal meat, the Mexican roofer covered in tar dust, the Turk and his wife who work in their restaurant sixteen hours every day? And where is the outpouring of reflection from children who are adopted, who want to be good, who want to be perfect for their new parents, lest they be returned to the store?

My own Umma told me that if she had kept me, I would have been either dead or a beggar. She told me the stories of how my father beat me about the head and my head turned black and blue, how he threw me from a window, how she was homeless and slept on the streets. How could a baby survive that?

My sisters gave me the chance to stay in Korea, when Umma was dying. As Jeong Kyong-Ah, I am a recognized citizen of Korea. I could have liquidated my apartment in the U.S. and just stayed. But I chose not to.

Would I rather have not been adopted? *I don't know.* The question demands that I calculate unquantifiables. How can I weigh the loss of my language and culture against the freedom that America has to offer, the opportunity to have the same rights as a man? How can a person exiled as a child, without a choice, possibly fathom how he would have "turned out" had he stayed in Korea? How many educational opportunities must I mark on my tally sheet before I can say it was worth losing my mother? How can an adoptee weigh her terrible loss against the burden of gratitude she feels for her adoptive country and parents?

When I watch the Mexican people in my neighborhood, I see what must be the backbone of a scattered people reaching out across the continent and binding them together. The backbone is many things: language, food, music, physical characteristics, religion, family. It must be the same thing that has held every immigrant group together in America until, after a couple of generations, the difference between Swedes and Norwegians or French and Germans wasn't so jarring anymore, and they married each other and only faintly held onto the customs that once bound them together, ensuring their very survival as a people.

As an adopted Korean, where is my backbone? How separated am I from the more than two hundred thousand Korean adoptees raised in the United States, Europe, Australia, and Canada? What can I salvage from this life, to teach my own children what I was never taught, about themselves and about the world and how to live in it?

> *Yahweh said, "Behold, they are one people, and they have all one language, and this is what they begin to do. Now nothing will be withheld from them, which they intend to do. Come, let's go down, and there confuse their language, that they may not understand one another's speech." So Yahweh scattered them abroad from there on the surface of all the earth.*
>
> [GENESIS 11:6–8]

Nearly a year and a half passed before I spoke with my American mother again. I call to tell her that Mark and I are engaged, and to talk. I hold onto my calm voice for as long as I can, and when it starts to shake, Mark pours me a drink.

"Well, I don't see how I can come to your wedding with all your friends talking bad about me."

"Mom, no one is talking bad about you. Can't we just be civil for one day?"

"Well, I don't think we want to come to your wedding if you have to try so hard to be nice to us."

"Mom, it wouldn't be complete without you. Mark and I really want you there. We're family."

"That's right. We are your family."

The unsaid words speak louder than what she says: they are my *only* family. Why isn't what I have been given in America good enough for me?

Four hours and a pyre of said and unsaid words later, what is left is uncertainty. I can only hope to understand my mother as a woman. If I put myself in her place, I see a woman who, when she was younger than I am now, adopted two girls and wanted to give them the whole pie, who before that was a girl herself with parents who gave her only crumbs. But she loved her mother, my grandma, anyway, and mourned her when she died. So we have that in common, this grief that we carry.

We also have this in common: our bodies, which remind each other of what we do not have, of who we are not. Mom, I am not from you; I will never be fully yours. I will never have peachy skin or blonde hair; I will never see the world through blue eyes. Could we accept each other if we were blind? Would we know each other by touch? Touch me here, Mom, in this place where I am sorry, where I love you, where I need to be healed.

There isn't enough fuel for anything to burn forever. Our silhouettes have been illuminated for a long time: this sharp, specific edge and that one, both unyielding. Now I feel the light around me burning itself out, giving way to something like forgiveness. Mom, if I were afraid, if I were lost in the dark, could you find me again?

People ask me how I know about my ancestors: "Everybody thinks they're descended from royalty or wealth. Do you have any proof, like documents or something?"

Well, not really. I have part of the family register, but not the whole thing. I have my own memory of visiting a decaying yangban house. But mostly, I have stories: what my Korean mother had told me about her parents, and what my sisters continue to say now that she is dead.

I count myself lucky because I have more stories and more documents than most. It's common for the agencies to tell adoptees that their documents were lost or destroyed or that there were never sufficient papers in the first place. Or, if they have the papers, they may have to "check with their lawyer" first before they can release the information, as if no one has requested the same thing before.

Who decided that the truth presented on official documents is more truthful than stories? Documents are only partial truths.

For instance, I bet that somewhere you could dig up a document that lists my uncle's dates of service in Vietnam. But those are only dates, and the full truth of it lies in his stories about cleaning out the helicopters. Another case: you could find documents detailing the ship and ports associated with one of my friend's ancestors, who came to America at the turn of the century. The truth lies not so much in these details, but in the story handed down—that she was a young woman who was so afraid of the men on the boat that she kept her boots laced for the entire passage, and when she got to America the boots had to be cut off her feet.

For that matter, even the "facts" on documents can be wrong. I have a document called a birth certificate that lists my parents as Frederick and Margaret Brauer: partial truth. (And although we were raised in the same family, my sister and I sometimes dispute what happened or was said during specific events: different versions of the truth.)

If I had to legally prove that my Korean family is my Korean family, I would be at a loss because the adoption agency won't give me the documents that fill in the crack between the time I was Jeong Kyong-Ah and when I became Jane Brauer. Even if I had them, who could legally prove that the baby in the photo is the same one they sent to America? It certainly wouldn't be the first time that children were substituted for each other: covered truth.

So, what remains through the rubble of the years is emotional truth, as fictional as it may seem.

Here's a story that's completely plausible and also completely false:

A Fairy Tale

Once upon a time, there were two Korean girls who loved their mother very much. But she could not take care of them. So she placed a smooth stone in the older girl's coat pocket and sent her daughters far, far away, to a place where people have more than stones to give.

In their new country, the girls grew healthy and strong. Their adoptive parents loved them very much, and they honored the girls' Korean heritage as they grew, helping them to remember the things they had forgotten. Together, they rediscovered Korean language and food, clothing and customs. They proudly displayed in their home the gifts sent by the Korean mother. Most importantly, they talked about the Korean family and made them a part of their own family. In their prayers at the dinner table, they asked God to bless their food, their family, and their extended family in Korea.

In school, the words of other children hurt, but those words stopped when the parents asked the teacher if they could make a special presentation in the classroom about the people and culture of Korea, so that the other children would understand and tolerate differences and accept the girls as friends. The teacher thought it was such a good idea that the whole school celebrated the different heritages of its children for the next month.

The children whose ancestors were German and Norwegian brought in old photos of their great-great-grandparents and recounted the family stories of the old country and long travel on ships. "Tell it again," squealed the children, when there was a story about a boy who threw up all over from seasickness or a story about a horse thief who hopped a ship to escape imprisonment.

"My name means Church on the Hill," one child said proudly. Another said, "My name means Bright City, and we still have cousins in Germany."

At home, the stone from Korea was given a special place on top of the butterfly shadow box. Sometimes, when her daughters were sleeping, the American mother held the stone in her hand and closed her eyes, trying to picture the land that made her daughters.

The two girls never felt ashamed of their heritage. They felt proud to be both American and Korean, and when the day came that they were old enough to travel back to their mother country, their American parents came with them, to see the strange and wonderful place that they had held dearly in their hearts and imaginations for so long.

In Korea, the two families met, and they exchanged gifts. This time, the older daughter held a different stone in her coat pocket, from a lake in America, and this she gave to her Korean mother so she, too, could touch a piece of America. The American parents met the Korean mother, sisters, and brother, as well as all the nieces and nephews, aunts and uncles, and extended family. The Korean family was just as big as the American family. In many ways they were the same. They made plans to meet again.

When the Korean mother became sick and died, the American mother invited the daughters and the rest of the family to a memorial service in her church, to honor the woman who was so important in the family's life. All the American aunts and uncles attended, and so did people who never met the Korean mother but who knew her as part of the family.

And when the daughters finally had their own children, both the American family and the Korean family rejoiced, for they knew that they were bound together in a way that would be celebrated and told for many generations.

The End

When she was a girl, my mom had sold chickens she raised on her parents' farm, then used the money to buy a broken player piano; the action still worked even though the player mechanism did not. Then she convinced the milk truck driver to give her a ride into town each week for a piano lesson; her own parents were too busy or unwilling to drive her half an hour each way. What she retained from all the trouble of raising chickens, selling them to be butchered, buying a piano, and hitching rides was one simple song: "Doctor, Doctor."

The interest was there but apparently not the ability, or, more likely, the time: she already knew the difference between necessity and luxury, and she used her time to do the important things: babysitting her four younger siblings while her mother was milking in the barn and learning to can vegetables, to sew a whipstitch, to cook chokecherries into syrup, to scientifically remove stains with vinegar or salt.

By the time I was old enough to notice the piano, Grandpa had already moved it into the garage, next to the farm machinery, where old oilcans and jars of nails accumulated on the lid. It saw several cars come and go, kept company with deer hides, and gradually lost its power to attract children.

Where the piano lives now is anyone's guess, since the farm was sold years ago, after Grandma and Grandpa died. Maybe the new owners of the farm did what farmers do: hauled it into a field to decay, just as they leave old cars and machinery in archaeological heaps. I like to imagine the piano has a new life out there, where a bird will occasionally sit on a key, pressing it so that the color of that particular patch of alfalfa turns B-flat, or maybe the wind reaches into the body and sings the strings alive again, like an Aeolian harp. More likely, no one touches my mother's piano, and no one thinks of the chickens that paid for it.

The odor of slaughter covered the farm every year during the last hot days of August. Processing chickens was a family affair, involving Grandpa and Grandma and all the aunts, uncles, and cousins.

First, we prepared the machine shed, setting up huge, empty copper wire spools flat side down as tables. We lined the garbage pails with plastic bags, carried buckets of cold water, set up hooks on wires to hang the carcasses. In assembly-line fashion, we killed and cleaned and packaged. I was the gizzard girl, not skilled enough to pull out the feathers or separate the guts but useful for removing stones from gizzards, rubbing the warm flaps clean and chucking them into a pile. At the end of the day, there would be a dozen chickens in each family's deep freeze, enough to last all winter.

This annual ritual, at the time boringly insignificant, would gain its importance after the memory itself had almost faded. Through the lens of memory, a depressed and self-absorbed college girl could see the symbolism of a chicken—whose head had been *thunked* off on a stump with Grandpa's ax—running around in circles, scritching out what appeared to be mandalas in the sand, singing a death song through its neck. John the Baptist came to mind as the dogs yapped and growled and the headless body finally wound down, collapsing in a heap of feathered transcendence.

I wanted my head to be removed, a metaphor so strong that only later did I realize that it was not a death wish at all. I dreamed about it, fantasized about it, imagined the mercy of a guillotine. My body was separated from my mind in a dualism so ridiculous that I almost flew apart at the shoulders.

What I longed for was wholeness, for my body to be as white and Northern Minnesotan as my mind. I longed to be normal, to not have to emotionally excavate myself to find my place. I wanted to be like my normal cousins who took after their normal parents or grandparents, who inherited the family colons and noses, whose extended families were asked about at Christmas.

These days, the same memory of chickens takes on a different significance: love by feeding, love by doing and not saying, love given and received without question. It is love that is synonymous with duty, but love nonetheless. This is the quiet love of my parents, a love that provides for the body. For them, caring for the body is also caring for the soul, and that was good enough for their people for many generations. This love provides chickens in the freezer and potato salad, smoked fish in winter and a bottomless pot of boiled coffee.

What were my parents to know of the inescapable voice of generational memory, of racial memory, of landscape—if they had never been separated from their own people? What were they to know of a girl whose presence demanded more from them than they either had bargained for or were capable of giving? They did not know this emotion or the word for it—*han*—but nevertheless it climbed up from the other side of the earth, through the bottoms of her feet, through her legs and body like the columns of a building, and was crystallized in sadness at an impasse in the throat, where a new and forgetful life became a tourniquet.

My marriage certificate let me choose who I wanted to be. Just write it down.

Jeong, Kyong-Ah. Or Kyong-Ah Jeong? Jane Marie Brauer. Jane Marie Trenka. Jane Brauer Trenka. Jane Kyong-Ah Jeong Brauer-Trenka. I finally choose Jane Jeong Trenka: one name from each family.

I wear it like a scar and a badge, the same way others wear their names, adapting language to reflect reality. I deliberately choose my name, my clan, my place in the world as it has borne me and created me. I choose to wear my joy and my pain in these words that signify me, and from this name you will know who I am.

I am a late bloomer. By the time she was my age, Mom had already been married thirteen years. Mark and I have just celebrated our first wedding anniversary.

Yes, we irritate each other: he snores, and I leave half-empty coffee cups all over the house. Yet, now I know what it is to live with unconditional love every day. I know what it is to feel secure, to dream about a future. Mark loves me fiercely and gently at the same time; he makes me see myself as someone worthy of love. He does not so much complete me, closing a circle, as he opens the windows: suddenly, all things are possible.

Dear Umma, I think the best I can do to honor your life is to live mine well, to take for myself what you wanted but couldn't have: a husband who loved and honored you, your children safe beside you.

Can you see me now, Umma? Can you see that I want to live in double happiness, once for you and once for me? This happiness is my grown-up magic dust; I hold it to my face and breathe my message into it. I toss my hands into the air, and my happiness rises aloft on the wind like a beautiful, golden angel. My heart is clear and bright, and I know that somewhere you feel my happiness, too, and I am finally home.

玖

913

I have planted a paulownia
to coax the phoenix to come.
I wait but the bird is not lured by a tree
planted by an ordinary soul.
Only a slice of moon shines,
suspended on the bare branches.

[ANONYMOUS, TRANS. JAIHIUN KIM]

The next time I visited Korea, more than two years after I had last been there, I had a husband (and his expenses) to consider. I bought the latest edition of the *Lonely Planet* and began investigating cheap hotels and public transportation.

"Please do not go to any trouble for us," I e-mailed Eun-Mi's friend in Germany, who translated and then forwarded the message to my sister. "We will visit you in Pyeongtaek, then travel to Haeinsa by train and bus. We do not want to inconvenience you. We know you are very busy with your business and children."

I had envisioned my next trip to Korea to be the period at the end of a long sentence, a last breath, the coda that finishes a sonata. I had decided months in advance that the trip would be the final chapter of this book, and here's how it would go:

After painfully and dramatically mounting the steep stairs of Haeinsa temple, each one representing a sorrow of mankind, I would place my stone very carefully and meaningfully back in the same place where I had found it seven years before. I would reveal to the reader that Haeinsa is the place where all duality ceases and that

Haein Samadhi is a state of meditation in which an enlightened person sees everything in its true nature: I planned to be enlightened. As far as books go, as far as writing your own truth, it seemed like a pretty good ending: seeming and being resolved, a beautiful moment. The only problem would be how to write it so that the reader would dwell there just long enough to absorb the full profundity of what I would describe: the ultimate finding of true identity, undivided, tranquil, enlightened.

Eun-Mi responded to my e-mail: "Dear Sister. I will propose a schedule."

"Dear Elder Sister," I wrote. "Please do not trouble yourself. We only wish to go to Haeinsa, and possibly our brother's farm if there is time. We have only one week because of Mark's work."

"Dear Sister. Following is the schedule during your staying." Eun-Mi had concocted a detailed, whirlwind schedule that crisscrossed the country, including tours in English at all the major historic sites, plus a traditional wedding and honeymoon on Jeju-do.

I am thirty-one years old, almost half my mother's age when she died. On reflection, I think that life is always a surprise—never what I planned, but always better than I imagined.

Korea changes each time I see her. There is a jarring mix of westernization and adherence to tradition. Kolon Tourist Hotel is doing good business, as is Happy Chicken Restaurant. There are more McDonald's and Burger Kings, and now we have overweight people, formerly an anomaly. Yet folk villages, which celebrate the old ways, continue to crop up, and on the eve of the World Cup women in all manner of public positions, including those who worked highway tollbooths, were to be found in their hanboks. There were free translation services, accessible even from the back of taxicabs by a three-way phone call; potable water straight from the tap; and a proliferation of Western toilets with toilet paper in every stall.

Korea, traditionally xenophobic, had opened its doors to the world. My husband was thrown into the spotlight by a European television crew at our wedding at the folk village in Seoul. Assuming out loud that I didn't speak English, they wanted to interview him for their World Cup coverage. "How does it feel to get married in Korea?" they asked. "You're a long way from home." And the formerly shy schoolchildren had somehow morphed into giggling teenagers, instructed by their teachers to practice their English on foreigners. "Hi! Welcome to Korea! Where are you from?" They mobbed my husband as if he were a rock star. They posed for pictures with him and completely ignored me. Eun-Mi was mortified at their "rudeness," which Mark perceived as friendliness.

On this visit, my sisters spoke more English; I spoke more Korean (in present tense, one verb per sentence). Although we still used the dictionary for almost everything, communication was comparatively easy. Translators were varying degrees of helpful, and I came to appreciate my sisters' clear pronunciation of what few words they could say.

My four-year-old niece had just started taking English lessons. She could say *yes, no,* and *good morning.* She wrote the English word "rain" beside her name in Korean, simply because she could. My eleven-year-old nephew exclaimed, "Oh my God-a, dude!" as he rode a Ferris wheel with my husband, and Eun-Mi and Myoung-Hee continued to exercise and improve their English.

Still, we communicated mostly in the system that we had worked out on previous visits: a combination of broken English and Korean, pointing at the dictionary, and heavy usage of a notebook and pen. With the help of a crudely drawn map, I managed to muster in formal conjugation *When America to you visit? Here my house is. Here Mi-Ja house is.*

We ended our stay on Jeju-do, a subtropical island covered by fences and houses made of volcanic rock; black chunks of them piled one on top of the other, each such an irregular shape that it is obvious every house and fence is built by hand, one stone at a time. Alongside these black houses are wild azaleas and spotted ponies, orange trees and fishing boats, and an ocean, astonishing in its perfection, that reveals and hides the earth every day with the rhythms of the tide.

The tide leaves designs in the sand, ripples folding into each other like the sound waves of a bell. It offers seaweed and clams for the people of the island, whose ancestors emerged from three holes in the earth, whose traditional clothing is the color of persimmons. The earth gives and then takes back, gathering up its clams and seaweed, its sons and daughters.

On misty days on Jeju-do, the basaltic cliffs stand out in vertical lines against the sea and the sea blurs into the sky, more subtle than a watercolor painting. The horizon has disappeared; earth and sky become one.

Parting at the airport with crude language was anticlimactic. I practiced my phrasebook sentence over and over: *Sugohashyosoyo*. Thank you for your trouble. And then in three seconds, it was over, and I was left with nothing to say again. Eun-Mi and Myoung-Hee huddled around the dictionary and five minutes later turned the notebook toward me: *We hope happy and health of you, Mark. We will missing you.* Mark bowed very deeply, and I gave Eun-Mi a quick hug, telling her, "*Saranghayo*. I love you."

We walked through the glass doors to immigration, turning to wave one last time (careful to make a side-to-side motion to say goodbye, not an up-and-down motion, which is the gesture for "come here" in Korean), and the space between us grew larger by meters, then tens of meters, and kept growing until it again became the size of an ocean.

No matter how much Korea changes, no matter how at home or not at home I feel there, no matter how much I change, one thing will remain: Korea is home to my mother, and now she is buried on a mountain in a Catholic cemetery, her beloved Virgin Mary placed atop the headstone, watching, unblinking, six tiny ceramic musicians playing silently on their harps and trumpets on the bottom ledge. On the front of her headstone her name is written in the official Chinese, and her Christian name, Julia, is spelled in hangul. And on the back, her accomplishments and her sorrows, her great burdens and her joys: the names of her children, carved into the granite: Sung-Duk, Sun-Yung, Sun-Mi, Eun-Mi, Mi-Ja, Kyong-Ah, Myoung-Hee. We had pulled the weeds from her grave, placed silk flowers in the vase, and bowed: three daughters and one granddaughter in a row, the same coal-colored hair and mulberry-paper skin, all of the same family, all with the same legacy to carry.

Who can dispute what is carved in stone? The family remains. Despite everything.

We will missing you, Umma.

On the way back to the U.S., Mark experienced reverse culture shock for the first time. He had fallen in love with Korea and the polite people in it. But our journey back across the International Dateline (which would cause us to arrive in the United States ten minutes after we left Korea) was hosted by a Chicago-based flight crew.

On this particular airline, most Southeast Asian flights and Korean flights are routed through Tokyo's Narita Airport. So, planes leaving from Japan are filled with people from all around Asia speaking many different languages; however, all must fill out forms in English in order to enter the United States.

Our flight attendant, obviously frustrated with this situation, tried to solve it by straining her voice almost to the point of shouting. "*Visa? Visa?*" she asked as she passed out forms. She stopped at one row and raised her voice to people hidden from my view. I suppose they didn't know what the forms were for, and didn't know they could request a translator, since the announcement that translators were available was only stated in English. So, the flight attendant raised her voice again, and then again, until one of the other passengers helped. "Koreans," she mumbled as she passed our row.

Our Chicago flight attendant, frosted into brittleness, assumed that I was traveling with the Chinese man sitting next to me. After she served him his complimentary beverage and snack, she held up a carton of milk, looked at me, and said, "*Milk.*"

I'd like to buy a predicate.

"*Milk.*" She stabbed at the carton with her finger. *What? Oh.* I finally figured it out. She was *explaining* the word milk to me; she thought that's what I probably wanted because the Chinese guy sitting next to me must have been my husband (not the white guy sitting on the other side of me), and that's what he was drinking.

"*Coffee,*" I told her, and pointed to my empty cup.

Mark and I decided to ignore the brittle flight attendant and get our chicken or beef from the flight attendant working on his side of the row. I let *him* do the talking, since it's clear that he speaks English, just as I request *him* to pay for things in Korea, since it's obvious that he doesn't speak Korean, and how I make sure that *he* talks to immigration officers first when we go to the counter together upon arrival in America, since it's clear that he's born and bred American.

Two things. One: interracial marriage has its benefits. Two: my life is fundamentally absurd.

You can't schedule enlightenment and you can't buy love, but you can buy a certain degree of freedom. Mark never got his big raise or even a retirement plan, but we have a lot more money than Umma ever did. We have enough to keep our children when we have them. We have enough to travel to Korea to see our family. And although people have tried to hide what was mine, to prevent these reunions from happening, no adoption agency bureaucrat can ever take away my frequent-flyer miles.

Now, impossibly suspended in a 747, I am reminded of the people who have tried to reach the sky from their small place on earth: the families of the sons of Noah, who built the Tower of Babel, who were scattered for their crime; the people of Korea, who built granite pagodas. The highest pagodas are the most fabulous, nearly all built with an odd number of tiers and in a prescribed shape: the squares on the ground represent man's world, and then, moving upward, the square's edges are clipped until they are transformed into octagons, then circles, then finally a lotus flower at the top, symbolizing Buddha's world.

Here, far above the highest temple, the words of the English-speaking tour guide, Mi-Sook—"Grace for your convenience"—come back to me: *Don't look for the Buddha inside the temple. Look for him inside yourself. He is there.*

There is a legend in Buddhist tradition about a man who had so much faith in his beliefs that he challenged his oppressors to cut off his head, for surely they would believe him after they saw the miracle that would happen. So they cut off his head. It parted from his body with such force that it shot into the sky, beyond sight. And what came back down was not a head, but petals—of white flowers.

Eun-Mi's instructions were to have an eggi and then come back to Korea. Mark and I think it's crazy to bring an infant on a trip so long, but we know that Eun-Mi would do it, and she'd do it in high heels, too.

Sometime during the day-night-day cycle of our time machine/trans-Pacific flight, I fell asleep, trying to imagine my comfortable bed at home in Minneapolis and the faces of my children.

"Mama." The voice is high and clear. It is a child's voice that sounds like my own.

"Mama, come with us."

She is perched on Umma's back, wearing a hanbok of child's design: bright green skirt and rainbow sleeves. Light brown ponytails cascade from above her ears, and her slim jaw, an echo of Mark's, frames a mouth like mine. She blinks her round brown eyes at me, puzzling over my reluctance.

"Let's go. Hurry now, or we'll miss it," Umma says.

Umma squats down and places my daughter on the floor. I rise out of bed, and we join hands. My daughter's hand is smooth as chrysanthemum petals; Umma's hand is hot and plump, the way it used to be, and she holds on too tight, the way she always did. In our little circle, we rise through the pear-colored ceiling, through the attic, and through the roof. The streetlights fade as daylight breaks, and it is August, and the last monarch butterflies are drying their wings, stretching, preparing for flight.

We rise farther and farther in the sky, away from the buildings, away from the noise, away from the weight of people's desires, their worries, their disappointments. We are lifted by the reasoning of butterflies, who are not informed of their own impossibility or frailty, who act on some faint memory without asking why.

Now the butterflies have begun their migration, and we glide into their updraft, Umma in her sunrise-colored hanbok, mine covered in birds, my daughter dressed in her rainbow. The skirts and sleeves of our hanboks billow like ships' sails, and the ribbons of our otkorums flicker wildly. We laugh with the exhilaration of flight, the joy of it, the way it feels like tumbling in the middle of a kaleidoscope.

The wind is brisk on our faces; the sky is a jewel. The sun never sets, nor does it grow too hot or too bright. When we are tired, the butterflies swoop down like a living roller coaster, setting us into a cornfield to drink the sap of milkweeds. South past wetlands and prairie, past ponds and delicious flowers, farther and farther we fly, until finally we arrive.

The forest floor is shady and cool, blanketed in pine needles. My daughter gathers up her rainbow with her brown arms and legs and places herself in a damp package on my lap. Her hair, soft as lamb's ears, smells like stargazer lilies, and I can feel her little heart beating inside my own body.

On this mountain, the monarchs glitter in shafts of sunlight. They hang from fir trees in giant clusters, a cathedral of stained glass wings.

"Listen now," says Umma.

In the hush of the cathedral, I hear a gentle swoosh, like the sound of breath, like the lilt of the ocean. It is the voice of millions of butterflies, opening and closing their wings. They whisper the secrets of their journey as they settle in for their hard-won rest, waiting for what will come next.

Opening and closing.

Opening.

Closing.

Open.

Close.

Open...

Notes and Acknowledgments

Names of some people and places in this book have been disguised, and others have not. For their protection, I have changed all names—either the surname or the personal name or both—of my Korean and American family members. As my Korean father did not follow conventional naming rules during his lifetime, I also disregarded tradition when fictionalizing names. I tip my hat to my courageous Korean-adoptee friends by borrowing many names from them. Friends, I hope you will forgive my small alterations in capitalization and hyphen use, which I have made for consistency throughout the book.

I have spelled Korean names honoring the Romanization each person uses in real life. I have followed the new system created by Korea's Ministry of Culture and Tourism to Romanize place names. However, I did not consistently follow either the McCune-Reischauer system or the new system for dialogue. Instead, I have spelled words in a way that I hope is easily read by the native English speaker with no knowledge of the Korean language or the standard sets of Romanization rules, which include diacritics and unlikely vowel combinations. Westerners should keep in mind that Korean is written in Korean and that all Romanization systems have been invented for the convenience of those accustomed to the ABCs.

In creating my personal mythology, I have borrowed liberally from Eastern and Western sources. I ask the reader's tolerance in navigating this world in which the improvisation on tradition is at times deliberate and at times the mark of a foreigner.

Jane Jeong Trenka is my real name.

I owe a tremendous debt of gratitude to the following people:

The remarkable staff at Borealis Books, including Greg Britton, Ted Genoways, Kevin Morrissey, Will Powers, Ann Regan, and John van Vliet. Special thanks to my lovely editor, Shannon Pennefeather, for her unerring intuition and bulletproof logic.

Cathy Spengler designed a book which gracefully captures the spirit of the story. Your artistry and fidelity to the text is much appreciated.

I also wish to acknowledge Brian Boyd of Yeong & Yeong Books; Carolyn Holbrook and SASE: The Write Place; Catherine Jordan and the Blacklock Nature Sanctuary; Dave Klaassen and the University of Minnesota Social Welfare History Archives; Naurine Lennox and St. Olaf College's Department of Family and Social Work; Jerod Santek and The Loft Literary Center; The Jerome Foundation; and The Minnesota State Arts Board, funded in part by the National Endowment for the Arts.

I extend thanks to the many artists I have met during the course of this project, who encouraged me to write and made room for me at the feast. These generous and insightful writers took the time to read the entire manuscript and provide extensive written critique: Aimée Houser, Martha Roth, and Heather Zehring.

I am grateful to my piano students and their families for granting me flexibility and for providing me with the copious amounts of chocolate needed to complete this book. My special thanks go to Miss Liliana B., who knows all about butterflies.

I owe an incalculable debt to those who have instilled in me a life-long love of reading: the English Department at Augsburg College and Dave Goebel of "Harlow," who continues to hold tight to his faith in what great literature can do for high school students.

To friends far and near, past and present, thank you for guiding me where and when you found me. Thank you, Eric E. E. Oberg, for adding to the *jeong* in our home and for being all-around best man.

I extend my gratitude to my siblings for sharing their stories and for being part of mine. I love you more than I can tell you. To my

American sister: thank you for giving me one second chance after another, for saving me in so many ways.

To my husband: *Du bist die Ruh...*

Since the mid-1950s, an estimated 150,000–200,000 Korean children have been internationally adopted.

Dear Umma,

Please forgive me for writing this book. I do not wish to bring shame upon our family; I only wish to honor you in what American way I know how. I am sorry that I could not find the right words. If you can overlook their faults, please accept these stories as my simple gift to you.

정경아
April 2003